# WHAT GOD CAN DO
# FOR YOU NOW

## FOR SEEKERS WHO WANT TO BELIEVE

ROBERT N. LEVINE

SOURCEBOOKS, INC.®
NAPERVILLE, ILLINOIS

Published by Sourcebooks, Inc.
P.O. Box 4410, Naperville, Illinois 60567-4410
(630) 961-3900
Fax: (630) 961-2168
www.sourcebooks.com

Library of Congress Cataloging-in-Publication Data

Levine, Robert N.
  What God can do for you now : for seekers who want to believe / Robert
Levine.
      p. cm.
  Includes bibliographical references and index.
  1. Providence and government of God—Judaism. 2. Suffering—Religious
aspects—Judaism. 3. Faith (Judaism) 4. Faith and reason. 5. Skepticism.
6. Judaism—Doctrines. I. Title.
  BM645.P7L478 2008
  296.7'2—dc22
                          2008025808


Printed and bound in the United States of America.
BG 10 9 8 7 6 5 4 3 2 1

To my family, whose ever-present love opens my senses to God's love.

To my Rodeph Sholom family, which never tires of seeking, but acts as if they already have found God's purpose.

To my assistant and friend, Julie Standig, who partners with me in sacred work and who always cares so much.

# CONTENTS

# ACKNOWLEDGMENTS

I AM MOST GRATEFUL TO my incredibly talented, devoted literary agents and friends, Jane Dystel and Miriam Goderich of Dystel & Goderich Literary Management. They are very well acquainted with my previous books: *Where Are You When I Need You?: Befriending God When Life Hurts,* written to engender dialogue within families after three children in my congregation died in one year, and *There Is No Messiah and You're It,* my conviction that none of us can sit back and wait for others, even transcendent forces, to do what we were put on this Earth to do. Jane and Miriam strongly encouraged me to inspire God-belief on the side of the religious spectrum that is more likely to be more skeptical. Their total commitment to the person behind the project is rare and cherished.

My editor, Hillel Black, has taken a strong personal interest in this project and has made many valuable suggestions of substance and structure. I will never forget that his son stood on the pulpit of my congregation as a Bar Mitzvah just four days after 9/11 as we endeavored to make sense of God's will and human behavior.

That struggle continues for all of us, and I am so pleased that this extremely focused, perceptive editor supports this effort to understand the divine-human relationship and to respond.

Julie Standig has been my assistant and friend for ten years. As a committed, searching Jew herself, Julie goes over every chapter with her loving, discerning eye, giving generously of her research skills, technical abilities, and sound judgment. This project would have been so much harder without her dedication and her willingness to even work from home to meet our deadlines.

I am blessed with a clergy team that not only grapples together with theological issues but skillfully shapes religious services so that congregants may feel God's presence and make sure that the resulting relationships make a difference. They make me proud every day.

Congregation Rodeph Sholom has been our spiritual home for the past eighteen years. Rodeph Sholom is a community in the best sense of the word. Members are there for each other in times of pain and joy and avidly study the texts of our tradition to discover the meaning of life for themselves and what is expected of them to repair the world. Our lay leadership covenants with the clergy so that we can model the best of Jewish living. I love this congregation, which is very much my extended family.

My wife Gina and I are entering our twenty-fifth year of marriage. Uniting my life with hers is the best decision I have ever made, and she gives me the best of her love, sage advice, and support every day. Our children, Judah, Ezra, and Maya, have amazed us with their talent and humanity. We couldn't love them more. This book is written with them in mind.

# CHAPTER ONE

## Is There Any Way We Can Believe in God Today?

**M**Y RELATIONSHIP WITH GOD ENDED one Passover night. That Seder meal was in fact different from all others in a very real sense. In every previous year, as my grandfather chanted every Hebrew word from the chicken-stained Haggadah text, my cousins and I would distract ourselves from boredom and hunger with a variety of games and pranks. The Passover following my Bar Mitzvah, however, I started to really pay attention.

As the plagues descended upon Egypt, my consciousness snapped to attention. I felt genuine outrage when I read in the Haggadah that the God who heard the suffering from our people would "pass through the land of Egypt on that night and [would] smite the first-born in the land of Egypt from man to beast...I and not an angel, not a messenger, I and no other, will execute judgment."

To free the Israelites from Egyptian bondage, the Haggadah was saying *God murdered the babies!* Of course, the Passover narrative was not a new story to me, but somehow, that day, this divine retribution penetrated my senses as a startling revelation.

Perhaps I should not have been so shocked by my own reaction. After all, many reasons exist to harbor supreme doubts concerning the God we read about in the Hebrew or Christian Bible. You probably share some of these and could add your own healthy dose of skepticism. Here is a good starter list of reasons to doubt God's very existence:

- The biblical God seemed to have a close, direct, and personal relationship with scriptural heroes like Moses, Jesus, and Muhammad. God "spoke" to them all the time. In all my years, I have not had my first one-on-one with God. So, if there is a God, why doesn't He talk to us now like He talked to them?

- God appeared to have performed countless miracles thousands of years ago, like dividing the Sea of Reeds and engineering the virgin birth. Because God is on record as a performer of such highly unlikely feats and because, seemingly, they have ceased to take place in our day, God must not be around anymore to actively hone His craft.

- Life disappoints, sometimes in tragic ways. People who are pretty confirmed agnostics have made requests of God at one time or another. These petitions range from the rather inconsequential—help me with the science test that I did not study for—to the consequential—even though my son has a pretty lousy SAT score, I should have enough contacts to get him into the Ivy League school I attended, but one more letter of reference from a really high-up source can't hurt—to the truly momentous—"Please, God, save my father from suffering and death." When these requests are not granted, we often feel angry and betrayed. Asking "Why do bad things happen to good people?" rarely produces salutary results. If the answer is "It's God's will," God gets dissed. If the answer is "God did not come through," God gets dismissed. Either way, whatever belief we have been able to muster can disappear very fast.

- The state of the world hardly reflects God's love and care for us. There's a story told about a man who hired a tailor to make a pair of pants. Every week, he stopped in to find out how his pants were coming along, only to find they were not yet ready. Finally, totally exasperated, he blurted out: "I can't believe this is taking so long. After all, God made the world in six days, but you can't make a lousy pair of pants in six weeks."

    "Yes," the tailor replied as he slowly worked on his unfinished sartorial masterpiece, "but look at the world and look at my pants."

Take a good look at our planet. Terrorism, the war in Iraq, massive slaughter and genocide in Darfur, and other man-made atrocities are leading indicators of a world in need of a makeover or a miracle. If there is a God, why is His masterpiece such a mess?

The Holocaust is still the greatest challenge to the existence of God. The Bible says that God made the Jews His treasured people. If that is true, why were they selected for genocide? The Holocaust was so devastating to the Jews and their faith that little was written about this unbearable tragedy until 1958, when Elie Wiesel published a riveting account of his experiences at Auschwitz in his first book, *Night*. In this autobiographical account, Wiesel relates a poignant scene in which three people were hung in the assembly place—one being a child with a refined and beautiful face.

"Where is God? Where is He?" someone behind Wiesel asked...

For more than a half hour, the child stayed there, struggling between life and death, dying in slow agony. He was still alive when Wiesel passed in front of him. His tongue was still red, his eyes not yet glazed. Wiesel continues: "Behind me, I heard the same man asking:

'Where is God now?'

"I heard a voice within me answer him:

'Where is He? Here He is—He is hanging here on this gallows...'

That night, the soup tasted of corpses."[1]

Powerful narrative, powerful challenge to God and belief. This is the very package of theological doubts I carried with me through college, even through the year I spent studying at Hebrew University in Jerusalem. All through that period, I continued my observance of many Jewish practices: I kept kosher, observed holidays, and prayed regularly. Such practices gave me a structure, solid grounding beneath my faith. Candidly, however, that prayer was not usually directed to a powerful, transcendent God. Even when I had a sense of the divine during services, I felt God more as a searing presence inside, a force that would not be denied, a type of guiding power. Yet, I did not feel I could petition or even give thanks to this God because I had no real relationship with Him. That bond ended one Seder night years ago, and neither of us could yet find our way back to the other.

During those exciting college years of intellectual challenge, I was introduced to the rich theological diversity in Judaism and became aware of similar ranges of belief resident in Christianity as well. In a course on Jewish medieval philosophy, I was introduced to the rationalist approach, to a God attained through reason. Maimonides, the most renowned of Jewish theologians, believed as a matter of logic that every force in nature is always set in motion by another, but originally, there had to be one force with no antecedent source. This "Unmoved Mover," an eternal fact of nature to Maimonides, made the resulting chain reaction of astrophysical processes possible. He called that force God.

In the twentieth century, the brilliant rabbi Mordechai Kaplan introduced another rationalist philosophy, positing that God is not a supernatural force at all but is a natural force in the universe that infused the human spirit, inspiring us to become all we can be. Later, I met theologians who took the existentialist approach, which teaches that God can be discerned not through reason but only through experience. Martin Buber, the famed German-Jewish theologian, in fact believed that little could be learned about God through reason. God could not be studied; God could only be met in a relationship, one which is accessible to us in a particularly intense, focused way that Buber terms the I-Thou relationship. For example, when we utterly lose ourselves in the exquisite beauty of a sunset or when a child dissolves in tears in our arms and we sense nothing else except her pain and her need, these rare moments are I-Thou encounters. As soon as we are aware of our involvement in them, I-Thou moments cease. Every time we are in an I-Thou moment, God is there as well—as the Eternal Thou.

Each of these theological systems opened my eyes to the range of belief available to all of us. Thinkers far wiser than me have articulated theologies that not only radically diverge from tradi-tional biblical views but are also embraced as proper and authentic. In college, I discovered that no one has to believe in the omnipotent, omniscient Almighty to actually believe in God.

Learning these theologies, I was comforted, but I was not converted. None of these God-concepts could help restore the key relationship in my life that I had lost. Surprisingly, the road to reconnection with that God flowed through a story written by an esteemed theologian, Rabbi Abraham Joshua Heschel. Shortly after World War II, a man is sitting across from other passengers in a train steaming across Europe. He is wearing a suit, tie, and overcoat, with only the blue tattoo numbers seared on his arm peeking out from his white shirt. The man watched the passengers sitting across the aisle don the tallit, or prayer shawl Jews wear before morning worship, then slowly wind the black bands of tefillin on their arms and place the black box between their eyes as a "sign upon their hand and frontlets between their eyes." Then he observed as they chanted the morning prayers in a prescribed order, swaying rhythmically to the musical chant. For three days, he sat rigid, expressionless. Finally, on the fourth day, unexpectedly, he took his coat off and draped his own tallit around his shoulders, put on tefillin, and joined them in the prayer service.

Asked later why he had changed his mind, he stared off into space, then slowly replied: "I got to think about how lonely God must be. Look who He has left."

In key episodes of the Bible, God emerges at times as a lonely, frustrated figure. God took an enslaved people out of Egypt, brought them to the Sea of Reeds, and, with Pharaoh's army in pursuit, made their miraculous escape possible. The people praised God for a moment, then immediately started to complain about the food in the desert. Standing at the foot of Mount Sinai, they felt the powerful presence of God manifested by thunder, lightning, and the blast of the shofar. Yet, when Moses went up the mountain, they crafted the golden calf.

If God couldn't make the sale then, if the people who experienced these miracles personally couldn't know that there is a God in the world, is there any wonder that people like us often struggle? Believing in God was not easy back then and is not easy now. Needing help, we build structures: mosques, churches, synagogues, designated places where we hope to sense the presence of God.

In the Hebrew Bible, God asked us to build a portable sanctuary, which we would carry through the desert, containing an ark that would house the tablets of the covenant. On the ark cover, we should weld two angelic cherubim facing each other. The text then says that God would come down and meet the people between the two cherubim on top of the ark.

God would *come to meet the people*. What an incredible statement! According to tradition, the transcendent God would descend from a very high place to make contact with us. How astonishing that the God on high would travel this distance. How awesome that such a God would care about us! I have never taken such a meeting for granted.

From my years of study as a rabbi, I came to realize that God fervently, even desperately, is seeking a real relationship of shared responsibility with us. God wants us to find each other and make a pact—the covenant upon which all Western religions are based—which requires that each side contributes and benefits in a mutually supportive way. What this effort presupposes, it seems to me, is that we are interdependent. We succeed and fail together. Ironically, many people do not even attempt such a search, never mind a partnership. Even many who claim not to believe in God still blame God for everything that goes wrong in their lives while taking personal credit for everything that seems to go right. This is not only a logical inconsistency; it is a total cop-out. To blame God is to totally absolve ourselves for what happens all around us.

Trying to have a relationship with God means widening our horizons beyond the narcissistic, beyond our contention that if anything bad happens to us at all, there could not possibly be a God, toward a conviction that if we really open our eyes to the wider world, we will increase the chances of believing that God is at work in our world, all the while looking for us to partner in crucial divine-human endeavors.

In my judgment, God is present even in those places that engender within us the most fear and dread. When I was a student, I was the first rabbinic intern to work at Memorial Sloan-Kettering Hospital, the world-renowned cancer center. Every Tuesday, I would visit patients on my assigned floors, carrying the mantle of God that I was not yet comfortable wearing. Sometimes, I would arrive at a bedside after the patient had received a devastating diagnosis, and I was able to provide a sympathetic ear and warm hand to his or her cold reality. My confidence was severely undermined, however, on my third Tuesday: I knocked and entered the room of a middle-aged woman named Gloria Posner in obvious distress. That day, I never got the chance to discover any details about her life or her disease.

"Hello, Mrs. Posner. I'm Rabbi Levine."

"Rabbi, Rabbi," she kept saying as if she wanted to contextualize my place in her current nightmare. "Rabbi Levine, how wonderful! Thanks so much for coming! Now, go tell your God I'm in here and thank Him for nothing! Nothing!" The next thing I know, her bedpan was hurtling toward my head like a guided missile, prompting me to flee the scene so fast that my yarmulke flew off my head. Grateful for being intact, I never gave a single thought to retrieving my spiritual headgear. Skullcaps are readily replaceable, I reasoned, but not the skulls they rest upon!

The next Tuesday, I approached her room with understandable trepidation, but I knew that I had to confront my fears. Using the same entering ritual, I couldn't believe the reception I received. Gloria was sitting up in bed, makeup on, hair combed, her face relaxed, her lips parted in a broad smile.

"Hello, Rabbi. So nice to see you."

Never once did Mrs. Posner mention the incident that had taken place one week ago. She probably couldn't even remember everything that had transpired. Since then, many things had happened to create this new visage: her white count had improved, her pain medicines had finally started to help, and she could keep down some broth. Gloria now felt stronger, more optimistic, and more hopeful.

When I got up to leave, Gloria grabbed my arm and, with a look of urgency, asked, "Rabbi, will you pray for me?"

As a student rabbi, I was ambivalent enough about offering prayer to people who are suffering and who in many cases would die soon. Who was I to pray for them? But Mrs. Posner needed me.

How could I refuse? Immediately, I launched into the traditional Jewish prayer for healing: "May the One who blessed our fathers and blessed our mothers bless Gloria Posner with a full recovery..." Tears filled her eyes, and she mouthed the words with me as best as she could.

"I say to the doctors all the time when they are about to leave my room," she said to me after we concluded the prayer, "'May God be with you.' I think God is with them, and I think God is with you as well, Rabbi."

"Thank you, Mrs. Posner. I will cherish that as your prayer for me."

Mrs. Posner smiled, squeezed my hand, and then turned deadly serious.

"You think God wants to take me soon?"

"I think God wants you to live. God has brought you here to this hospital in order to join with all His partners—the doctors, the nurses, all of us—to give you every chance."

"What if nothing works?"

"You've done all anyone can do. So will the doctors, so will the rabbis, so will God. God cannot banish all death from the earth. That's why the Book of Ecclesiastes emphatically states that 'There's a time to be born and a time to die.' Death is a reality, Gloria, but we fight it off. We choose life as best as and as long as we possibly can. Even when life comes to an end, God is here to assure us that we are never alone. Our faith believes and so do I that your soul then leaves the body and that God will accompany your soul to the next realm."

"You think we're going someplace after this?"

"It is impossible for me to believe that all reality is merely what we humans can see and hear. I firmly believe that there are worlds beyond our own and that God will be there as well."

The next week, I found out that Gloria was able to go home and that she died soon after that. Her daughter wrote me a beautiful letter and told me that my pastoral visit that day gave her mother strength and peace of mind. As I read her words, tears came to my own eyes, and perhaps for the very first time, I felt like God's messenger here on Earth.

God is present in my view whenever and wherever we let the divinity in.

To open your mind to the possibility that God not only exists but cares about what happens to us and is an active force in our personal lives and in human history, suspend your doubts for a moment and consider anew what the world might look like from God's point of view. From that perspective, shouldn't God be more than a little disappointed with us? Far from getting the adulation and credit deserved for millions of years of brilliant service, God is being attacked as nonexistent or irrelevant by secularists and atheists on the one hand and glorified by fundamentalists as an all-powerful being to be worshipped and obeyed but not to be taken seriously as the demanding covenantal partner envisioned by all Western faiths.

Take the creation of the world. Some fifteen billion years ago, the universe burst into being in an astrophysical phenomenon dubbed "The Big Bang" by a bitter opponent of the theory, astronomer and physicist Sir Fred Hoyle. The electronuclear explosion led to a sudden, flaming-hot expansion, then cooling, followed by the attendant formation of atmospheric forces like gravity and electromagnetism as well as solid substances like atoms and molecules combining into stars and galaxies.

Arguably, all this could have come into being on its own. Yet, how, pray tell, did the universe formulate all the conditions necessary to permit the incredible evolution of species leading to the creation of man and woman?

The chances that this remarkably structured universe just burst on the scene without any transcendent plan or mind fashioning it are, as one wise cynic once observed, the same as an explosion in a print factory and the letters just happening to arrange themselves in such an order as to form the *Encyclopedia Britannica*. In the same vein, the celebrated zoologist Sir Julian Huxley once calculated the odds against the horse developing by evolution from a one-cell protozoan as one out of a number consisting of three million zeros. Just to write that number, you would need fifteen hundred pages!

You can explain Charles Darwin's theories of evolution for days on end, but I will never lose my sense of utter disbelief that a human being could develop from the fertilization of an egg by a single sperm. Explain all you want, but to me, it's still a miracle!

Enamored with science and technology, too many of us have lost sight of the miracle. Somehow, we believe that human beings have or will solve all problems and find answers to questions that have eluded wise ancestors for centuries. I continue to overcome such arrogance in my own psyche. For sure, I have become in awe of the fact that Jews are still here as a vibrant people practicing a living faith. The Bible records God's promise to Abraham that despite all the trials and tribulations ahead, Jewish survival is assured: "And I will establish my covenant between me and thee and thy seed after thee in this generation to an eternal covenant—to be a God unto thee and thy seed after thee." (Genesis 17:7)

Close to four thousand years later, there are no more Canaanites or Philistines, no more remnants of the mighty Roman Empire or the modern Third Reich. Through countless attempts to isolate, diminish, and eliminate Jews, Judaism and its people live! I can find no rational, historical, or sociological basis for why we have survived all these tribulations. Frankly, one of the strongest reasons I have to believe in God is knowing that this covenantal promise has been fulfilled. I cannot say with certainty that Abraham lived and surely don't think that God spoke to Abraham in human language, but the fact that we still occupy the world stage and are attempting to do God's will is strong evidence that God lives, God cares about us, and God still performs miracles in our midst.

If I have opened your mind to the possibility of a caring God operating in our world, that still leaves open the question of who is God
and what does God do in our universe today. It is clear to me that our
country is seriously divided on this question between those who
hold a fundamentalist point of view and those who hold a pluralistic
point of view. Based on evidence largely gathered from Scriptures
themselves, I will argue in this book that these are not equally legitimate theological expressions of faith. In fact, the fundamentalists in
our midst have seriously misunderstood who God is and what God
demands from us. The following scene is depicted in Jeffrey Sheler's
*Believers, A Journey Into Evangelical America:*

> Evangelical bishop John Gimenez stood before his fundamen-
> talist Rock Church in Virginia Beach, Virginia, one day after
> George W. Bush was re-elected as President in 2004.
>
> "I want to remind you, my friends, that the Lord is sovereign.
> It's the Lord who chooses who wins the election. The President
> didn't win because of the Republican Party, he won because of a
> group of people who went to the polls who believe in God, who
> believe in prayer, and who believe in moral values. He won
> because of the church, because of people who don't follow a
> party but who follow a man, the man Jesus Christ."
>
> "Amen!"
>
> "Glory to God!"
>
> "We're going to recover everything we've lost in this country.
> We're going to stop the killing of babies. We're going to put
> prayer back in our schools. We're going to protect the family.
> We're going to turn away from the sins that beset us as a nation."
>
> "Yes!"
>
> "Amen!"[2]

Of course, these pastors do not claim to simply speak for themselves, to be advancing their own political views or personal

status. They are speaking in the name of the Lord, claiming the Holy Scriptures as their absolute and literal authority.

To fundamentalists, life as supplicant comes with an instruction manual—the Holy Scriptures, the Word direct from heaven. As Sheler puts it, "their faith is simple and sure: the Bible is God's word inspired and infallible from cover to cover, and it points to Jesus as the only way of salvation."[3]

Although the flock has its marching orders, what in fact saves these followers from their sinful and slothful ways is the grace that comes from accepting Jesus, the expiating savior for all humanity, who made the supreme sacrifice of dying for their sins. What is expected of these faithful is wholehearted acceptance of the risen Christ and the self-love that comes from having the burden of sin lifted from their shoulders. In the meantime, they can feel the satisfaction of having been saved and can spend all their free time condemning those who have not been saved to eternal damnation. As the website for famed pastor Rick Warren's Saddleback Church clearly spells out: "Only by trusting in Jesus Christ as God's offer of forgiveness can man be saved from sin's penalty" and "To be eternally separated from God is Hell."

The fundamentalist God clearly does not love all humanity, is not pluralistic, and has no tolerance for differences. Even though the Bible is constantly alluded to as the unquestioning authority for their point of view, make no mistake about it: This is not truly the God of Scriptures but is the God of pastors like Rick Warren, James Dobson, and Pat Robertson.

Too many of us think: "Well, they must have God on their side. They must have Truth on their side. If only we did." The real Truth is that their depiction of God is the supreme being they wish they could find in Holy Scriptures but cannot. Their God prefers that we save our own souls rather than save the bodies and souls of others. He is the false God the Bible constantly warns us against embracing. Ironically, they share a God-concept with the atheists, who need to posit an equally extremist, wrongheaded view of God in order to debunk it: the atheists and fundamentalists should talk more often so they could discover that they view God in the exact same way.

Both miss the Bible's clear view that the world was created with two power centers—the human and the divine—and we will either succeed or fail together. That is the very reason why the covenant was established. God didn't just create the world and walk away; He remains a powerful force for good. Human beings were created so that together we could do what we cannot do alone. When we are powerless or indifferent, God can also be defeated.

This is precisely why tragedies like the Holocaust and Darfur occur. Our failure to harness this powerful coalition for good means that forces that wish to bring salvation and hope to the world can be defeated. In my view, there are many random tragedies in the world. To my way of thinking, a good God does not order a plane crash or a tsunami. But the Holocaust or Darfur cannot be called acts of nature or random tragedies in any way. Responsibility must be assigned.

I can't tell you whether God was originally an omnipotent being. Even if that was the case, God clearly gave up on omnipotence in the drafting of the agreement between the human and divine realms we call the covenant so that we can be potent. Free will was given so that human beings could decide whether to be moral or immoral, involved or indifferent. When human beings decide to destroy each other on a massive scale, there is probably little God can do. As an active and powerful force for good, God's might can be activated to wonderful ends by human beings, and conversely, that force can be weakened and defeated by human resolve or diffidence.

So, during World War II, the combined forces of good were devastated by an overwhelming evil: the Third Reich. Our job is to learn from that defeat, for all of us to do better the next time we are confronted with evil. The covenant posits our interdependent relationship. When we rouse ourselves for action, we energize God's power. When we rekindle our faith in God, we are inspired to do more to repair the world.

If we are created in God's image, we possess much ability to carry on this battle.

Rabbi Hugo Gryn was sent with his father to a work camp by the Nazis. Conditions were grim, and starvation-level food rations were distributed daily. As Chanukah approached, Rabbi Gryn's father was determined to find a way to celebrate the miracle of God's past intervention in history. He wanted to find a way to kindle light. So, he took precious margarine rations, molded them into candles, and used threads of cloth for wicks.

"Why are you doing this, Papa?" Hugo asked.

"You must eat to keep up your strength," his comrades pleaded.

"In this place," he replied, "we have learned that you can live two weeks without food, two days without water, but you can't live two minutes without hope."

Hope is necessary for human beings so we can marshal our collective will and harness God's will to truly make a difference. We cannot rewrite history, but we can rewrite the destiny of those suffering now amidst unspeakable conditions all over the world.

In no way can I give you a precise formula for how much what happens in our world is God's doing and how much is ours. No human being will make that calculation. But many believe this covenantal relationship has been in force throughout the length and breadth of human existence. Most likely, it is the reason why we are still here as people of faith. There is much we can do together.

So, we cannot fully know who God is or discover our relationship to the divine by reading the Bible. The scriptural records of such important relationships may inform and inspire us; however, we have to build our own ongoing, dynamic relationship with God and endeavor to assist each other in mutually dependent ways. I do believe that sometimes the Bible is not accurate in its depiction of God's role in the world. It is our job to correct the historic record through our own beliefs and our own actions. The one truth I rediscovered over the years is that the God I believe in demands justice and our best effort to promulgate human dignity. The God I know, in fact, would have done virtually anything to free Israelite slaves from Egypt. Plagues to break the will of the Egyptian monarchy seem like appropriate weapons against the despot. The death of Egyptian soldiers or slave overseers may be justified as painful means to an important end. But in my theological view, *God never sanctioned or perpetuated the killing of babies.*

Biblical authors who saw all goodness and tragedy as God's will perhaps couldn't have thought otherwise. Many babies were dying—God must be responsible.

We can think differently. People with faith can know otherwise. At least, let us stop dismissing the possibility of God's existence and goodness because of abject cruelty toward the most defenseless people in our midst, all attributed to God. Perhaps our sources are guilty of faulty intelligence.

As I began to rebuild my relationship with God, I was comforted by the fact that in a number of theological systems, God and people continue to find their way back to each other. It is probably no coincidence that Heschel's first book was called *Man Is Not Alone* and the second was called *God in Search of Man.*

How does God search for us? How can we ever really search for God? The prophet Isaiah shows us the way with words that are so vital that Jews read them in the synagogue at the height of their fast on Yom Kippur morning:

You seek me daily and strive mightily to know my ways? You say: "we have fasted and you have not noticed. We have afflicted our souls and you have no knowledge of our efforts?"

16

I'll tell you why I haven't noticed your fast—it simply has not produced the results I am looking for. Your fast has done nothing about strife and contention in your world. You have not fasted in a way that makes your voice heard on high.

You want to fast in a way to make this an acceptable day to the Lord? Then know what I want you to do:

Is not this the fast I have chosen?

Is it not to deal thy bread to the hungry, and that you bring the poor that are cast out into thine own house?

When you see the naked, that you clothe them and that you not hide yourself from thine own flesh and blood?"

In my own congregation, Rodeph Sholom here in New York City, members walk into our beautiful sanctuary on Rosh Hashanah and find a simple brown paper bag on their seats. They are asked to fill the bag with food and bring it back on the holiest day of the year: Yom Kippur morning. So, even before they hear Isaiah's thundering prophecy, they will have already put their bag of sustenance on a truck, which City Harvest will use to help feed the almost one out of five children in this country who live beneath the poverty line. God has every right to be angry, and we should share His outrage that the richest country in the world permits so many human beings in our midst to go hungry. In that same bag, congregants find notices to volunteer in our homeless shelter and countless other opportunities to fulfill our potential as truly human beings.

How do we find God? Not by sitting around and parsing theological arguments.

You want to find God?

The Bible's simple answer is to start doing: Feed the hungry. House the homeless. Clothe the naked. Teach kids to read. Soothe the ill. Comfort the bereaved.

When you do what God would do if standing in our midst, when you act godly, you will find God. Really.

Many people will still say that rather than God creating us, we created God because we simply need to have a divinity in our lives. I don't share this view; in fact, it strikes me that everything that can be said about our need can also be said about God's. God may have created us precisely because God needed us to make this world all that God wants for us but cannot do alone. To give up on this mutual search is to assert that there is no transcendent plan or hope for humanity, that we have no reason to behave morally, except for public opinion or sanction.

But there are many compelling reasons to behave well and to believe in God.

You will still encounter many of your doubts in this book because they have been mine at one time or another. However, I am too much in awe of human beings and our capacity to repair our world to accept such a fate. The potential for tragedy exists everywhere, every day, but so does the potential for miracles. Thus, I will continue to build my relationship with God so that together we can create miracles.

Thousands of years of human civilization and progress have given us reason to believe that as we deepen our search for God, God will respond by searching for us as well. This book will show you the way.

# CHAPTER TWO

Faith for the Faith
Challenged

**M**ERYL SEEMED MORE RELAXED THAN usual.
Just before December vacation, she visited my
study in obvious agitation, crouched in almost a
fetal position. "I don't even know what happened
to George," her husband for the past twenty-four years. "He was so
docile, so quiet. All of a sudden, he's drinking, coming home at all
hours, yelling, screaming, and bullying me. When I say anything
in my defense, he looks at me with eyes filled with such venom.
He looks like he wants to smack me. I am afraid for my life."

"How does he relate to Charlie and Dylan?"

"They hide in their room when he comes home. He never even
asks about them, never even wants to kiss them good night as he
always used to. I hear them crying late at night. They're afraid of
him. They're afraid of what's going to happen to them."

That early December day, Meryl looked like she was falling apart, along with the rest of her life. I tried so hard to get her to seek help, to find shelter for her family. Meryl dutifully took the cards containing the essential phone numbers that I was certain she wouldn't call. Clearly, she wasn't ready to make such a move. Paralyzed by the shocking turn of events in her life, Meryl couldn't find the energy or motivation within herself to do what she needed to do to protect herself and her children.

"Call me anytime," I told her, pressing my cell phone number into her wet palm. "I mean it, Meryl. Don't wait until it's too late."

Three weeks later, Meryl was sitting in the same chair in my office, looking like a huge burden had been lifted from her shoulders. "The moment the kids were out of school, I scooped them up and we went skiing out west. You know, Rabbi, something happened to me up there. It was as if God was talking to me on that mountain—'Meryl, you've got to do something. You've got to get rid of that guy. Don't worry. I'll be there for you.' The feeling was surreal, but when I got down and got home, I knew what I had to do.

"When I told George, he broke down crying, sobbing really, but I was strong. God was with me at that moment. Now he keeps calling, promising me everything. I said: 'Don't promise. Just do it.' But I'm not going to rush to take him back. The kids seem so much happier. Dylan is laughing again. Charlie has stopped bed-wetting, and I'm actually looking forward to the sun coming up in the morning."

Notice that Meryl had her experience with God not in the Rabbi's study or in the pew but on top of a mountain. Notice, too, that this was not just a lovely, isolated feeling of rapture. Her encounter with God on that mountain filled her with resolve to do something about her troubled life. What Meryl discovered up there was nothing short of a revelation from God, helping her to discover her inner strength and inspiring her to meaningful action.

Students of faith shouldn't be shocked by such occurrences. Examples abound in the Bible: Abraham found out the meaning of faith when he was stopped by the angel of God from sacrificing his son Isaac on Mount Moriah. The prophet Elijah defeated the Canaanite god of Baal on Mount Carmel. On Mount Tabor, a courageous military and political leader, Deborah, mustered her courage and troops to again battle the Canaanites. On Mount Nebo, Moses could only look out over the Promised Land that his descendants would enter without him.

All the main characters in the three major Western religions— Judaism, Christianity, and Islam—had major life-changing faith experiences on a mountain. Poet William Blake was surely right when he wrote, "Great things happen when men and mountains meet." In fact, what happened to these three superstars of Western religion on those summits determined the shape of each of their faiths. Moses was summoned to the mountaintop to put into words God's commanding revelations concerning how his charges should believe and how those beliefs had to be translated into an action plan that could produce a society of civility, morality, and justice. According to the Book of Exodus, Moses heard God's commanding voice on a mountain and translated what he heard into the Torah: a set of commandments that would forever change the people's relationship with their God and with each other.

The New Testament doesn't tell us whether Jesus was summoned to a mountain or went there to escape the teeming crowds and crackling political tension of Rome-dominated first-century Palestine. Perhaps he ascended to get his thoughts together. Perhaps he needed God's reassuring presence before he could go back down to do his prophetic work. Chapter 5 of the Gospel of Matthew simply says, "Seeing the multitudes he went up on a mountain." Perhaps he couldn't stand seeing so much human pain and want. More likely, he needed divine reassurance and sought the confirmation that only a mountain could provide. Upon those heights, he felt empowered and further aided by the communal warmth of his disciples gathering around. Only then could he open his mouth with words of blessing:

> Blessed are the poor in spirit,
>     for theirs is the Kingdom of Heaven...
> Blessed are the meek,
>     for they shall inherit the earth.
> Blessed are those who hunger and thirst
>     for righteousness...
> Blessed are the peacemakers,
>     for they shall be called sons of God...
> Blessed are those who are persecuted for righteousness
>     for theirs is the Kingdom of Heaven...
> Blessed are you when they revile and persecute you and
>     say all kinds of evil against you falsely for My sake.

Clearly, Jesus of Nazareth needed all the inspiration he could muster because he was trying to motivate what he perceived to be a downtrodden and persecuted people to seek not just political freedom but spiritual freedom. This required a change of behavior, even a transformation of the Torah's traditional norms and ethical prescriptions, in order to gain entrance to the messianic world Jesus terms the Kingdom of Heaven.

Handsome and charismatic, Muhammad cut a familiar figure in the bustling city of Mecca. Muhammad was not happy with the material obsessions of the populace he saw around him. His spiritually focused friends were more concerned with personal salvation than social reform. However, Muhammad was seeking a new spiritual path. Accompanied by his wife Khadijah, he made an annual trek up Mount Hira during the month of Ramadan, dutifully distributing alms to the poor who visited him in his mountain cave. His experience in the year 610 was dramatically different, however, than at any other time. Soundly asleep in the cave, he was jolted awake by a heavenly voice telling him he was God's messenger.

"I was standing, but I fell on my knees and crawled away, my shoulders trembling," he recalled. "I went to my wife Khadijah and said, 'Cover me! Cover me!' until the terror had left me." Thinking he was possessed by an evil spirit, he was beside himself with despair. Suddenly, the mysterious figure reappears, presenting himself as the angel Gabriel, who immediately pressures Muhammad to recite.

"What shall I recite?"

The angel does not answer but instead grabs him in a vice like embrace and squeezes him until Muhammad hears God's words coming out of his mouth.

> Recite in the name of your Lord who created you
> From an embryo He created the human
> Recite your Lord is all giving
> Who taught by the pen
> Taught the human what he did not know before
> The human being is a tyrant
> He thinks his possessions make him secure
> To your Lord is the return of everything[4]

The resultant long string of revelations together with those that would come to the prophet over the next three years were grouped into Suras, or chapters, known as the Quran, or the Recitation. This revealed wisdom affected the theology, private demeanor, and public responsibility of the prophet, his disciples, and his followers ever since.

Why are all Western religions born on a mountaintop? Apparently, it is hard to hear God's voice, sense God's presence, surrounded by people who are too busy to stop and listen, those who are obsessed with self, who have no room for belief. Raised in Pharaoh's palace, for example, surrounded by legions of fawning officials in Egypt, Moses never experienced God. Alone in the desert, however, he responded to the commanding words coming from the burning bush. On Mount Sinai, Moses may have received the Torah, but coming down and viewing his people building the golden calf, his faith was as shattered as the tablets.

Ironically, faith, which must be made manifest in the real world, helping real people to have any real value, is often hard to find in that very setting with its many pulls, problems, and distractions. Moses, Jesus, and Muhammad discovered this and retreated in order to listen better and to learn what was to be their spiritual purpose in life. Many people do the same today. Some go on meditation weekends or yoga retreats. More than a few rabbis I know spend a period of days together sitting in silence in order to experience everything at a deeper level—trying to taste their food, work on their ability to concentrate, think and feel without outside distraction, and, in the process, trying to sense the presence of the transcendent, ineffable God.

Some find the silence helpful, some unbearable. But whether they develop a deeper feeling of holiness and a better relationship with God may very well depend on what they bring to the retreat. Clergy who have too healthy an ego, who feel they have it all together, who love to hear the sound of their own voices, won't hear any other voice, whether they sit in silence on the beach or stand in Times Square. In my experience, to find faith, you must be needy in some way, vulnerable, open to the helping and healing that a deity can bring. A member of the Cheyenne Indian Nation wrote a prayer in this vein:

O Great Spirit, whose voice I hear in the winds,
And whose breathe gives life to all the world, hear me!
I am small and weak, I need your strength and wisdom.

Let me walk in beauty, and make my eyes ever behold
the red and purple sunset.
Make my hands respect the things you have made and my
ears sharp to hear your voice...
I seek strength not to be greater than my brother, but to
fight my greatest enemy—myself.
Make me always ready to come to you with clean hands and
straight eyes.
So when life fades, as the fading sunset, my spirit may
come to you without shame.[5]

Where and when, then, can we find faith? When I did a tour
for my first book, *Where Are You When I Need You?: Befriending
God When Life Hurts*, I would often ask those attending a book
signing if they had ever had an experience with God. A surprising
number raised their hands. So, I asked if they had experienced
God in a house of worship? A few. During a sunset, on a mountaintop, or standing before the ocean? A few more. When their
child was born? Some more hands. When you suffered a devastating blow, like a death? Hands flew up in the air so quickly, I
was stunned.

As soon as their memory banks were opened up, these people
were eager to tell me their story of faith. One woman talked of a
tornado that reduced her house to rubble. "We didn't have much
to begin with," she said quietly, holding back tears. "Everything
Jay and I had was now gone. Funny, as we were picking through
the rubble, I heard this voice telling me everything would be
okay, you still have each other, don't give up.

"I just know God was talking to me. God just wouldn't let me
quit, and I didn't. Jay died two years ago, but since that day, I
know that I am not alone. God is with me. I am not alone!"

One day, I walked into the sanctuary and Mary was there. Quite
often, she would sit quietly in the back of the sanctuary. Usually,

I just let her be, but one day, I slid in next to her. Mary glanced over, shot me a welcoming smile, but quickly turned serious:

"My Sam loved it in here. He would always talk about coming to shul with his grandfather, who would tell him stories of the old country and remind him of his responsibility to his heritage and faith. Somehow, Rabbi, my faith lived through Sam. Now that he's gone, I try to feel it, but I simply don't feel very much. I come here to feel closer to Sam and all he believed."

"Come with me, Mary," I said, motioning her to follow me onto the bimah, the high prayer platform. At that moment, I had no specific plan other than I wanted Mary to come closer to what Sam had felt. When the ark was opened before her, Mary let out a slight but audible gasp.

"I've never been this close."

"Would you like to hold a Torah?"

"The Torah? I...I never have. No one has ever asked me to."

"I'm asking."

"Could I?"

Holding the Torah in her hands, Mary began to weep. She caressed the red velvet cover, kissed the scroll as if she were kissing Sam, and even began to sway as if she were having a religious experience.

That day had a profound effect on Mary. "I can't explain it," she said, "but I felt Sam and God standing right beside me, and they sort of lifted me up, gave me strength, hope, faith even. I'll always be grateful, Rabbi, for what you and they gave me that day."

I often think about Mary, eyes closed, tears flowing, swaying with the Torah. Physical movement helped her find faith that day. Many other days of swaying came to mind as I thought back to the times I sat in services next to my grandfather, watching the old men, heads covered with their prayer shawls, swaying to the rhythm of prayer. I had always thought that these guys were so pious that they had to express what they already knew and felt through body motion. Now I wonder whether in fact they all did believe so fervently. Maybe they swayed or shuckled, in the Yiddish, out of habit or tradition. Perhaps they shuckled in order to find their faith so that even if they were riddled with doubt, they could leave the rational behind in favor of a physical experience that might produce positive spiritual feeling.

Movement, actual physical activity, is part of prayer, as old as prayer itself. The Israelites broke out in ecstatic dance in praise of God after being saved from Egyptian enslavement. Ecstatic fervor and movement possessed followers of Jesus when "they were all filled with the Holy Spirit and began to speak in other tongues as the Spirit gave them utterance." (Acts 2:4) It is impossible to passively sit through a Gospel or Evangelical worship experience. Pulsating music produces as much body movement in these services as you'll find in an aerobics class. Prostration before Allah, of course, is a staple of Muslim prayer. The prophet Muhammad was reported to prostrate himself in mud and water. According to one of his disciples, "With my own eyes, I saw the Prophet, upon completion of the morning prayer, depart with his face covered by mud and water." (Sahih Al-Bukari, Hadith 3.235)

Visit a Hasidic shteibl or the Western wall, and you will find Jews swaying fervently in an effort to climb the seven spheres between the human and divine realms. Rhythmic music is used in all sects of Judaism and Christianity. Even in the Conservative Rabbinic School at the Jewish Theological Seminary, what used to be staid prayer has become for many "Jam Davening," which is "part guided meditation, part sing-along, part traditional prayer, and part dorm-room musical jam that includes instruments ranging from guitar to didgeridoos."[6]

Carolyn Stearns wrote a very moving article called "The Song Finally Sung." Here is a brief excerpt:

My friend Cynthia contracted leukemia ten years ago. I interrupted my performing career and teaching obligations as a dancer and went from Connecticut to California to teach her what I knew about dietary changes and visualization as tools to combat the disease. She listened carefully to all I had to say, but finally rejected my message. She chose to stay with more traditional forms of therapy..."Do you ever pray?" Cynthia once asked.

"Yes, dance is my form of prayer."

"Dance?" she exclaimed.

"Yep!" I answered. "I haven't knelt or closed my eyes or pressed my hands together since I was a little girl."

"Why not?"

"Because that kind of prayer doesn't comfort me."

"Nor me," she said wearily as she looked out onto the water. "I wish now, though, that I could pray, I think it would help."

"I think you're right..."

"Will you show me how you pray?"

"I wish I could. Unfortunately, I can only do this kind of praying when I am alone."

"But I'm your best friend!"

"I know!...When I dance to pray, I need to get real quiet inside myself, so quiet that I don't even know when I start to move. If any one is watching me, I automatically start performing..."

Suddenly, without a word, Cynthia stood up and walked down to the water's edge. In that moment she displayed more energy than I had seen since my arrival...

I watched and listened with amazement as she paused and threw her arms up toward the sky and shouted, "Okay God, if you're up there, now's your chance to teach me to pray!"

Cynthia looked so frail standing there, the wind whipping her trousers around her thin legs, her hands looked translucent as they reached toward the sun. And then without any warning or discussion she started to sing.

Oh my how she sang! She sang a song that came from a place deep inside her that sounded very old...As she sang, I cried,

FAITH FOR THE FAITH CHALLENGED

because for the first time I could imagine her flying away.

When Cynthia stopped singing, she turned to look at me with the same delighted smile I saw when she rode her two wheeler bicycle for the first time before...I'll remember that smile forever.

Cynthia's singing was constant during the remaining three weeks of her life. It created a magical energy that made her soul glow, even though her body grew weaker and weaker.

I believe the energy she received through her singing released the fear that kept her from letting go of her pain and kept her from dying. Once I heard the quality of her song I knew she'd be fine—better than fine. Though it was only a question of time until she died. I felt as if she had received what she had been looking for her whole life.

Cynthia was still alive when I said my final goodbye.

"Goodbye, dear friend. Thank you," I whispered.

I'm not sure she heard me. She was quietly humming a song, a song that was ushering her back into the life of spirit. When her singing stopped, she squeezed my hand and was gone.[7]

A related technique that builds fervor is the use of the mantra, constant word repetition. This Navajo prayer chant illustrates the technique:

House made at dawn.
House made in evening light.
House made of the dark cloud...
Restore my feet for me...
Restore my body for me.
Restore my mind for me.
Restore my voice for me.
This very day take out your spell for me...
Happily may I walk.
Happily, with abundant dark clouds may I walk.

Happily, with abundant showers may I walk...
May it be beautiful before me.
May it be beautiful below me.
May it be beautiful above me.
May it be beautiful all around me...[8]

The Hebrew liturgical prayer, the Kaddish, is most familiar to many as a mourning prayer. In the face of a great loss, often devastating grief, Jews utter a prayer that offers effusive praise of God using a succession of verbs recited in mantra like fashion:

Yitbarach v'yishtabach veyitpaar veyitroman v'yitnasei, veyithadar veyitaleh veyithalal shemei dekudesha—God's holy name is to be blessed, praised, glorified, exalted, honored, elevated, and sanctified.

As you pronounce each Aramaic word, you will notice that the praises are alliterative. Surely, most people coming to prayer services after a stunning loss do not feel like uttering words of praise to God. Their faith is more likely to be shattered than it is likely to be intact. Over the course of weeks and months, however, the mantra plays on the mind and heart, moving us to a new place. Slowly, our outlook may improve, darkness turns to light, emptiness to hope, fatalism can turn back to faith. Kaddish recitation is an active aid in the process of faith restoration.

The reason Kaddish can work, then, is that a new perspective can eventually emerge for a person during the grief journey, a sense that a supportive God, not the egotistical self, is at the center of the universe. Coming out of pain, I am more humble and grateful, more aware that there is more to my life than perhaps I realized before, a new purpose.

The story is told about a Japanese youngster who wanted to be a karate champ. He traveled across Japan to the school of a famous martial artist.

"What do you want from me?" the master asked.

"I wish to be your student and become the finest karate champion in the land," the boy replied. "How long must I study?"

"Ten years at least," the master answered.

"Ten years is a long time," said the boy. "What if I studied twice as hard as all your other students?"

"Twenty years," replied the master.

"Twenty years? What if I practiced day and night with all my effort?"

"Thirty years," was the master's reply.

"How is that each time I say I will work harder, you tell me it will take longer?"

"The answer is clear," said the master. "When one eye is fixed upon your destination, there is only one eye left with which to find the way."

In the faith journey, we realize that the way itself has value and that it can lead to a different destination than we had ever planned. The way can lead you back to the very people and places we purport to cherish but rarely take the time to savor. Wiesel captures this in the Hasidic story of a man named Eizik, who is so poor that he worried day and night. There was rent to be paid, the butcher, the tutor, there were daughters to clothe and marry, what was he to do? He continued to pray.

One night, he had a strange dream: He saw himself swept away to a distant kingdom, to a capital city under a bridge in a shadow of an immense palace. And a voice told him, "This is Prague, and over there the palace of the kings, and now look, for under this bridge at the spot where you're standing, there is a treasure, it is waiting for you, it is yours."

In the morning, Eizik dismissed his dreams. But that night, as soon as he closed his eyes, the very same vision came to call. The voice asked: "Don't you want to be rich? Would you rather stay worried your whole life?" Next morning, he woke up and said, "Go to Prague?" What an idea, he had no desire to go there, he didn't know anyone in Prague, it was so far away, so expensive to get there, and he had no money. But the next night, Eizik heard the voice: "You haven't left yet?"

Worn down, he decided to obey. He started the journey on foot. A few weeks later, he arrived in Prague, famished and exhausted. He recognized the river, the bridge, the palace, but it was not a dream. He saw the very spot under the bridge that looked oddly familiar. What should I do? I could dig a hole, take a look? What do I have to lose? But the bridge was guarded; the soldiers must not become suspicious. When he got there, the captain of the guards accused him of spying. Too frightened to invent a story, he told the absolute truth: the dreams, the worries, the long walk from Krakow, the constant voices. He was convinced that the officer would call him a liar and order him shot. But the captain actually burst out laughing.

"That's really why you came from so far away? You Jews are even more stupid than I thought. If I was as stupid as you, if I listened to my voices, do you know where I would be at this very moment? In Krakow. Yes, in Krakow. For weeks, this voice at night has been telling me there's a treasure waiting for you at the house of a Krakow Jew named Eizik, son of Yekel. Yes, under the stove. Can you see me going from house to house turning down all the stoves, searching for a nonexistent treasure?"

Of course, Eizik wasn't punished. He hurried home, moved the stove, and found the promised treasure. He paid his debt, saw his daughters married, and built a synagogue that bears his name, Eizik, son of Yekel, who remained pious even when he was no longer poor.

The point of the Hasidic tale, of course, is that our greatest treasures are right before our eyes if we only look for them. They are right in front of us, right below us, if only we look in the faces of people precious to us and remember to thank God for our manifold blessings.

The ability to be able to feel blessings is another vital prerequisite to finding faith. If need is essential for faith, so is gratitude. Perhaps it is true that you have to have faith in something—yourself, other people, the institutions that frame your life—in order to have true faith in a higher power. Faith leads to faith.

Let's be honest: All of us would much rather live with faith than without it. All of us need belief, sometimes desperately. Faith gives us a perspective we wouldn't have otherwise. That old Peggy Lee song sometimes plays through my mind: "Is That All There Is?" Is that all there is? Without faith, we might have no larger goals beyond selfish pursuits. The world becomes a narrow, darker, more dispiriting place. As Rabbi Milton Steinberg puts it, men cannot live "joyously, hopefully, healthfully, perhaps not at all, without it...The God-faith...illumines the darkness within ourselves. It dispels the misgivings lest our strivings serve no purpose, lest our ideals be mere idiosyncrasies...instead our aspirations come to be seen as refractions of God's purpose, our struggle as elements in the working out of the divine scheme. Finally, the God-faith sends us out into the battle for the good in ourselves and society with heightened morale. We know, as we join issue with the forces of evil, that we do not fight alone."[9]

Most importantly, with faith, we come to see ourselves as needed, as God's partners, without whom God cannot succeed in this tumultuous world where much conspires to defeat the good. If you truly have to be needy to secure faith, as I argued earlier in this chapter, so too do you need to feel needed.

Faith found on a mountaintop or in front of a Torah or within ecstatic prayer has to send you back into the grimy marketplace where human need resides in order to have true meaning, in order to really matter.

When the children of Israel were commanded "You shall be holy, for I, the Eternal God, am holy," holiness was defined as having only a small component of ethereal spirituality. For the most part, holiness was defined as leaving your cushy schmooze with God and returning to the world to make sure that the poor are fed, the workers are paid, and those who are enslaved are liberated. When Dr. Martin Luther King Jr. delivered what turned out to be his thunderously powerful final sermon at a church in Memphis, Tennessee, on April 3, 1968, he spoke these memorable words to the congregation:

> We've got some difficult days ahead. But it doesn't really matter with me now because I've been to the mountaintop. And I don't mind. Like anyone, I would like to live a long life; longevity has its place. But I'm not concerned about that now. I just want to do God's will. And He's allowed me to go up to the mountain. And I've looked over. And I've seen the Promised Land. I may not get there with you. But I want you to know tonight that we, as a people, will get to the Promised Land..."

Keep in mind that the reason he was in Memphis in the first place was to fight for sanitation workers who were denied the right to strike. King had been to the mountaintop, but now he was down among those who make their living collecting smelly garbage, fully engaged in the battle for workers' rights and human dignity, a decent wage for garbage workers, a long way from the heady and isolating splendor of the mountaintop.

So, we can sit on the mountain and wonder if God really is speaking to us. The truth of the matter is we will never really know for sure. But if we take that moment of connection and turn it into many moments of connection with the people God has created, loves, and wants you to love, you will much easier find that solid faith you have always been looking for. You will be doing God's work, and, very possibly, much doubt will soon disappear. Take it on faith until you roll up your sleeves and act. After a while, you will no longer have to take it on faith.

The student came to the rabbi and said: "I did a wonderful mitzvah today. A man came to me who was starving, and before I gave him food, I taught him all the proper blessings to say." The rabbi looked at him and said: "You meant well, but you did not act well. When someone comes to you in need, you must act as if there is no God in the world."

"No God in the world?" The disciple could not believe what he was hearing from this most pious teacher.

"Yes. When someone comes to you in need, you must act as if no one, neither God nor man, can help except you."

"But, Rabbi, what about his neshama? What about his soul?"

"Take care of his body and, therefore, you will take care of your soul."

That is what we must do. In taking care of their body, we'll find our soul and, most likely, our faith.

A man takes a tour of his final resting place where the angel meets him and says, "I want to show you both hell and heaven."

The angel first takes him to hell. Beautiful, wooden doors swing open to a bountiful banquet with long tables filled with the most sumptuous food. People sit at the table but look miserable. No one is eating.

"This is hell," the angel says, "because the people are not blessed with elbows. Their arms are stiff and though the best fare imaginable sits in front of them, they are tortured because they simply can't get at it."

"Now let me show you heaven." He takes him to another huge hall. The wooden doors swing open to what appears to be the exact same room; long crowded tables are filled with delectable food.

"I don't understand. These rooms seem identical. Same people, same food."

"So it seems," the angel intoned. "But here the people have found the will and way to pick up the food and feed each other."

Faith is that will and the inspiration to find the way, the way to nurture their body, your soul, and the world which lies well below the mountaintop, the world that we and God must continue to build together.

# CHAPTER THREE

## The God of the Atheists and the Fundamentalists

LTHOUGH I SUSPECT THAT MOST people don't know exactly what they think about God, there are two groups of true believers who have no ambivalence. Atheists and fundamentalists, in fact, should be soulmates. They share a lot more than either would care to admit, as both present a remarkably similar portrait of who God is and how God operates in the world. Moreover, they share a core understanding of what real people will do in the service of that deity. The only difference is that one wants us to swallow that faith without question, while the other unquestionably finds the same faith impossible to accept. Frankly, both scare the living daylights out of me. Neither group would want to share a pew. In fact, if it were in their power, they might not want to share the same planet.

While atheists and fundamentalists may not want to share a room, they sometimes share the same skin. That was the case with Jonathan, who came to my office with his parents for their pre-Bar Mitzvah appointment. With every upcoming Bar or Bat Mitzvah, I dialogue with my students about everything from what is their favorite subject in school to what baseball team they love and then how they best connect to their religion.

Invariably, the conversation comes around to their theology. Do you believe in God, I ask, and, if so, what is your God-concept? Very few thirteen-year-olds categorically reject the existence of God. Those who do will say something like: "I don't believe in God, I believe in science." On the other side of the spectrum, a considerable number of students have strong belief in an all-powerful God, much as the Bible portrays. Those in the middle sometimes speak of God as a spirit or force within that inspires them. Jonathan came to my office armed with the first draft of his Bar Mitzvah speech, which featured an all-powerful God leading the people out of Egypt, a divine warrior who divided the sea and wiped out their common mortal enemies.

"Do you believe in an all-powerful God, Jonathan?" I asked.

"Actually, I don't believe in God at all, Rabbi."

"But you talk about God here as an omnipotent military leader without whom the Israelites would not be saved and without whom we would not be here today."

"I know, Rabbi, but that God isn't around anymore. There's no evidence that God is so powerful today. Probably God could do everything He used to do, but God doesn't seem to want to, so I don't believe in God anymore."

Clearly, the God whom Jonathan doesn't believe in really is a fundamentalist God, the God who is all-powerful and not to be questioned. I suspect that he has a lot of company in our country, but truth be told, there are a number of people in all Western faiths who believe without a scintilla of doubt, and that belief is central to their identity and how they live their lives.

Christian fundamentalists, who usually prefer the term *Evangelicals*, literally believe in the portrayal of God presented in both the Hebrew and Christian scriptures. Their God is an omnipotent being who created the world in literally six days, no more and no less, fashioned us in His image, and sent down to Earth an aspect of self. Jesus Christ is made manifest both to show the world its messianic potential and to make it possible for people born in the state of original sin to shed that sinfulness through the wholehearted embrace of he who died on the cross for those sins. This God surely can be caring and compassionate, but make no mistake about it, He rewards those who achieve salvation and severely punishes those who do not. More ominously, say many evangelists, God is involved in an ultimate war of good versus evil against those who would undermine His power and mission in the world and ultimately must go down in the apocalyptic battle to take place at the End of Days as we know them.

If you have any doubt that Evangelicals hold those beliefs, consider reliable research on these matters:

In a December 2004 *Newsweek* poll, the question was asked: "Is the Bible literally accurate?" Eighty-three percent of Evangelical Protestants said yes, but only 45 percent of Catholics felt likewise. When asked "What do you personally believe?" 94 percent of these same Evangelicals believe in God and 75 percent believe in Satan or the devil. A 2002 CNN-*Time* magazine poll asks: "Will the world end in an Armageddon-type battle between Jesus Christ and the Antichrist?" Seventy-one percent of Evangelical Protestants said yes.[10]

For Evangelicals, such "good news" is to be shared because, simply put, they need to evangelize. In the words of Christine Rosen, author of the book *My Fundamentalist Education,* their job even as young students was to "open their eyes" and to turn the darkness to light and from the power of Satan unto God that they may receive forgiveness of sin.[11]

39

Of course, the only ones who are so forgiven are those who hold the precise same faith as the Evangelicals. They have the Truth, they know it, and want to spread the word about these central tenets of the Evangelical faith—the Bible is God's inerrant word; having a personal relationship with Jesus Christ is the only way to salvation; Christians are obligated to share the good news of salvation with others.

All three Western faiths have their core beliefs, their foundational myths, their orthodoxies. Plenty of right-wing Jews also believe they have the Truth and no one else does. So do fundamentalist Muslims, who not only believe that every word revealed to the prophet Muhammad comes directly from God but also that their explanation of those words is the only correct interpretation.

These orthodox or fundamentalist groups share the belief that their adherents, and only their adherents, will achieve salvation. In each of these apocalyptic views, it is not the warm, compassionate, loving God who will save the truthful; rather, it is the bloodthirsty, take-no-prisoners, vengeful God who will wipe away all but those with the right kind of faith—namely, people who hold the precise worldview that fundamentalists hold dear.

The Hebrew prophet Malachi strikes that type of strident tone:

> For behold the day cometh that shall burn as an oven, and all the arrogant and all who do wickedly shall be reduced to stubble. The day that cometh shall burn them up saith the Lord of Hosts. Thou shall leave them neither root nor branch. Unto you who fear my name shall the sun of righteousness arise with healing in his wings...Behold, I will send you Elijah the Prophet before the great and terrible day of the Lord. And he shall turn the hearts of the fathers to the children, and the heart of children to the fathers lest I come to smite the earth with total destruction. (Malachi 3:19–24)

The New Testament's Book of Revelation presents a view of Christ that is more militant than many are used to. Here, Christ is the mighty warrior routing the enemies of God:

> Now I saw heaven opened, and behold a white horse. And the Christ who sat on him was called Faithful and True. In righteousness He judges and makes war. His eyes were like a flame of fire...He was clothed with a robe dipped in blood, and His name is called the Word of God. And the armies in heaven clothed in fine linen, white and clean, follow Him on white horses. Now out of His mouth goes a sharp sword, that with it He should strike the nations. And He Himself will rule them with a rod of iron. He Himself treads the wine press of the fierceness and wrath of Almighty God...Then I saw an angel coming down from heaven...He laid whole of the dragon, that serpent of old who is of the Devil and Satan and bound him for a thousand years...Now when the thousand years have expired Satan will be released from his prison and will go out to deceive the nations which are the four corners of the earth, Gog and Magog, to gather them together to battle: whose number is as the sand in the sea...Fire came down from God out of heaven and devoured them. (Revelation 19:11–15; 20:1–10)

Let me assure you that these are not long-forgotten biblical passages. As the CNN poll revealed, the vast majority of fundamentalist Christians believe that Armageddon is just about to happen. Lest you think that these numbers are exaggerated, consider one of the great publishing phenomena of the twentieth century, a group of novels laying out in graphic detail what will happen in the End of Days called *Left Behind,* a series which sold some sixty million copies in print, video, and cassette formats.

In these books, the evil Antichrist, who rose to power through the United Nations, one of the fundamentalists' most despised institutions, was headquartered in Iraq, not far from the Baghdad of Saddam Hussein. In these books by Tim LaHaye, the Tribulation Force fought shoulder to shoulder with and in the name of God.

In his book *American Theocracy,* Kevin Phillips makes the point that by September 11, 2001, the *Left Behind* series provided extraordinary context and at least a subconscious motivation for President Bush to go to war. The distinctions that mattered to secular Americans—that Saddam Hussein was not involved in the 9/11 attacks; that the weapons of mass destruction excuse for invading Iraq was specious—would not have mattered much to the tens of millions of true believers viewing events through a *Left Behind* perspective.[12]

Frightening end-of-life scenarios are part of the fundamentalist school curriculum as early as the fifth grade. That is when Rosen's class learned about what was supposed to soon happen in this world. In the End of Times would come great tribulations—seven years of violence and disaster in which at first Christians would be brutally persecuted. The Antichrist would emerge and lead the armies of Gog and Magog (Magog is later transformed from the location of Gog's kingdom in biblical times to Gog's evil ally) in an invasion of Israel, thus beginning Armageddon, the ultimate war between good and evil. At war's end, Christ would return to Earth triumphant. Many of God's chosen people will be slaughtered, while the righteous remnant would repent and recognize Jesus as Messiah. All good Christians would join God in heaven, returning to Earth only later to assist in ruling during the millennium. The scooping up of the righteous into heaven was called the Rapture.

All this was meticulously charted by Rosen's class, which took these prophecies literally and learned how to spot the signs of the End of Days. If Rosen and her classmates took End of Days prophecies seriously, her mother was even more rabid in antici-pating that day. For example, she once threw the family television off the balcony in order to escape the Antichrist's "subtle seduction." Dutifully, she bought the family Rapture-related T-shirts and posted a bumper sticker on her car—"Warning: in case of Rapture this car will be unmanned." If her mother's actions were unnerving, the movie that the fundamentalist schools showed these impressionable young students, graphically displaying the slaughter of the unfaithful together with the Antichrist, provoked downright panic.

After the screening, amid the shocked silence of the chapel, the principal went to the podium and asked if students wanted to be "left behind" to be tortured or tormented or if they wanted to accept Jesus and be raptured. Students were encouraged to come to the front of the auditorium, where the principal asked, in a booming voice, "Are you 100 percent certain in your belief?" Weeks later, some kids were still experiencing serious nightmares following the movie and the intimidating aftermath.[13]

Such an image of God could fill any potential believer with utter fear and dread. Fundamentalists seem to want to keep their adherents in ideological line, lest they miss the Rapture. Clearly, the goal is to scare people into submission and compliance. This is not a God with whom you enter into any sort of relationship. This is a God before whom you quake in terror and do all you can to prepare for the end.

How can people embrace with joy a theology that brings such suffering to virtually all God's children? Equally hard to fathom is belief in a God who encourages people to achieve their salvation at the total expense of those who suffer an ignominious death. The End of Days is coming, say the fundamentalists, and you better grab the spiritual lifeboat offered to you so that you will be swept up to the heavens and not out of the world altogether. Such certainty. So little time.

Living among us is yet a second group of people who also possess the Truth and know it! Atheists know who God is and are flooding the markets with books proclaiming such certainty. Titles like *God Is Not Great* by Christopher Hitchens, *The God Delusion* by Richard Dawkins, and *The End of Faith* by Sam Harris leave little room for ambiguity. What is important for this purpose is that the God they introduce in order to totally debunk is the most bloodthirsty, autocratic, and immoral of creatures. Not surprisingly, theirs is the God of the fundamentalists. They want to present that image of God because it allows them to set up an absurd straw man and spend thousands of words bringing the divine down from the heavens and turning that God into a horrendous figure.

Dawkins begins with an all-guns-blazing assault on the biblical God:

> The God of the Old Testament is arguably the most unpleasant character in all fiction: jealous and proud of it; a petty, unjust, unforgiving control-freak; a vindictive, bloodthirsty ethnic cleanser; a misogynistic, homophobic, racist and infanticidal, genocidal, malevolent bully.[14]

Dawkins covers himself after this screed by claiming that he will not make it easy for the rest of us by using that image of God. Rather, he will attack the superhuman/superintelligence who designed the universe and everything in it. Yet, in chapter seven, Dawkins savages the God who personally commands Abraham to sacrifice his son and who chooses to slaughter those who built the golden calf. Speaking of the Binding of Isaac, Dawkins writes: "Apologists even seek to salvage some decency for the god character in this deplorable tale. Wasn't it good of God to spare Isaac's life at the last minute?" Concerning the punishment of the golden calf–builders, Dawkins writes: "Then he told everybody in the priestly tribe of Levi to pick up a sword and kill as many people as possible. This amounted to about three thousand which, one might have hoped, would have been enough to assuage God's jealous sulk. But no, God wasn't finished yet."[15]

Atheists spend little time on Christian or Jewish End of Days scenarios because they are otherwise focused on Muslim End of Life fantasies. As Harris put it: "We must not overlook the fact that a significant percentage of the world's Muslims believe that the men who brought down the World Trade Center are now seated at the right hand of God amid 'Rivers of Purest Water'...These men who slit the throats of stewardesses and delivered young couples with their children to their deaths at five hundred miles per hour—are at present 'attended by boys...in the kingdom blissful and glorious.'"[16]

Harris seems to believe that the God he doesn't believe in is capable of sitting around honoring Islamic terrorists from 9/11 simply because they believe they were performing their unspeakable acts at the explicit encouragement of the entire divine realm.

That being said, all the top atheists publishing today spend precious little time actually talking about the God they wish to take down. Their true obsession is not with God at all but with what some remarkably unstable people choose to do in the name of God and their religion. For example, the full title of Hitchens's book is *God Is Not Great: How Religion Poisons Everything,* but he does not tell us very much about his views on God but, rather, what people do in God's name.

For his part, Harris tells us that Muslims are "utterly deranged by their religious faith"[17] and that millions, maybe hundreds of millions, of Muslims will be willing to die before they would allow someone else's version of compassion to gain a foothold on the Arabian Peninsula.

Leaving aside the question of how Harris would defend such outlandish statements, I still contend that he is telling us little about God and everything about some fanatical people. The most absurd and desperate stretch is Dawkins's multi page assertion that Adolf

Hitler was no atheist but was clearly influenced by his Christian upbringing with its medieval history of persecuting and hating Jews. So, contends Dawkins, there is no way that Hitler could be driven only by a wholly secular, racist, national-socialist ideology.

Why do these guys feel they have to link every monstrous human evil to God? Do their arguments not have sufficient strength that they have to rush Hitler and 9/11 to the fore? This reminds me of the story of the clergyman who wrote in the margin of one of his sermons—argument weak here, shout louder next time! These guys seem to be shouting in evermore desperate tones as they run out of sane things to say.

Let me respond with declaratory sentences to Dawkins, Harris, Hitchens:

GOD IS NOT RESPONSIBLE FOR ALL THAT PEOPLE DO IN THE NAME OF GOD. RELIGION IS NOT RESPONSIBLE FOR WHAT PEOPLE DO IN THE NAME OF RELIGION.

The God of the atheists, like the God of the fundamentalists, is an ogre, always willing to impose His will at the expense of human life and dignity. Clearly, they need to present the most extremist of gods because that God poses the most tempting target. Even then, they spend almost all their time attacking adherents of that God, not God himself. Interestingly enough, they don't even understand the faith they purport to eviscerate. For example, Dawkins thinks that "Faith is an evil precisely because it requires no justification and brooks no argument."[18]

Has he even read the Bible? Moses required so much justification for God wanting to destroy the entire people after some had fashioned the golden calf that God changed His mind and spared the innocent. The Book of Job is all about God's need to justify divine actions to human sufferers.

God brooks no argument? Abraham screams at God, "Shall the judge of the whole earth not do justly?" (Genesis 18) Abraham then gets God to agree to spare the cities of Sodom and Gomorrah if some righteous people can be found within their borders.

The bottom line is that the God on display in the Hebrew and Christian bibles is more complex than Evangelicals or atheists will acknowledge. Obviously, they want to keep it simple-stupid so that, in the former case, you will unquestionably obey, and in the latter case, you will unquestionably walk away.

What is fascinating is that these atheists have many questions and are hardly immune from the same sense of wonder that is the root antecedent of faith. Dawkins paradoxically states: "Think about it. On one planet and possibly only one planet in the entire universe, molecules that would normally make nothing more complicated than a chunk of rock, gather themselves together in terms of rock-sized matter of such staggering complexity that they are capable of running, jumping, swimming, flying...and falling in love with would-be chunks of complex matter. We now understand essentially how the trick is done, but only since 1859. Before 1859 it would have seemed very, very odd indeed. Now, thanks to Darwin, it is merely very odd."[19]

Still, Darwin has not diminished Dawkins's propensity for wonder. What was very, very odd is now just very odd. Unwittingly, Dawkins is making a most compelling case that some larger force made these processes possible. Clearly, all the scientific analysis in the world still leaves Darwinian evolution and his theory of natural selection far less explainable and still quite a bit of a mystery.

Harris's concluding words in his epilogue to *The End of Faith* are equally stunning:

"Man is manifestly not the measure of all things. This universe is shot through with mystery. The very fact of its being, and of our own, is a mystery absolute, and the only miracle worthy of the name.... No personal God need be worshipped for us to live in awe at the beauty and immensity of creation."[20]

Harris is in awe! After spending an entire book making mince-meat of those who are similarly stunned, Harris here concurs with the reasons why people believe and provides no other explanation for the mysterious and miraculous all around us. Because Harris can't make a cogent case, he feels the need to make increasingly insulting comments and analogies. "If we ever do transcend our religious bewilderment, we'll look back upon this period in human history with horror and amazement. How could it have been possible for people to believe such things in the twenty-first century?...The truth is, some of your most cherished beliefs are as embarrassing as those who sent the last slave ship sailing as late as 1859...I would be the first to admit that the prospects for eradicating religion in our time do not seem good. Still, the same could have been said about efforts to abolish slavery at the end of the eighteenth century."[21]

Because Harris has nothing more convincing to say, he wants to equate those who believe in God with racist owners of slaves. Dawkins and Harris simply want us to abandon the apocalyptic, cruel warrior who brooks no human argument. Hitchens has an alternative. He calls for the New Enlightenment, a renewed faith in people to do temporally what others only hope to accomplish spiritually.

What is wrong with his proposal is that we all remember the failed promise of the old Enlightenment. Faith in human beings has not seemed terribly justified, given the fact that we just lived through the bloodiest century in the history of humankind, one that included the Holocaust and 9/11.

Let's get this straight: Atheists carry around the same sense of wonder and mystery faith adherents do, have less than total faith in science, and have a far less convincing blueprint for a just and moral society than people of faith do.

My Bar Mitzvah student Jonathan provided an insight that both Evangelicals and atheists should internalize:

"Maybe the reason God isn't doing so much in the world now is that He expects us to make the world better." Jonathan seems to be saying that the God he doesn't believe in actually believes in us and thinks that we can do God's work. I share his view that belief in God has to matter, not only to our personal lives but to the world we all share. The God who cares about us, who has expectations that we will care about things beyond ourselves, is a most compelling deity.

Atheists may very well share a God-concept with the fundamentalists. Yet, not only is that God-concept not appealing to the modern searcher, but it does not even keep faith with the biblical God. Theirs is not the God of Scriptures. That God wants us to use our rational minds to relate to the deity, wants us to find our morality within the divine-human relationship, wants us to partner with God through covenant to fight the good fight, not in an apocalyptic end of days battle but in an everyday effort to repair this fractured world.

That crucial relationship between God and us is predicated on the hope and expectation that we will neither abandon faith in God or faith in ourselves. That is a God-concept that Jonathan may come to embrace. I already do.

# CHAPTER FOUR

~

# God's Big Bang: Why Science Needs Religion

STANDARDIZED TESTING IS A FRIGHTENING fact of life and probably as hard to prepare for as death and taxes. These days, ludicrously expensive testing services try to cram as many vocabulary words and algebraic equations into the less than fully developed brains and psyches of students at every grade level along the stressful journey toward the schools of their or their parents' choice.

When I was in high school dreading the SAT, we were told by the Educational Testing Service (which we regarded with the same degree of awe and disdain as many view the IRS today) that there was really not much we could do to prepare. Read the handy little booklet, sharpen your No. 2 pencils, and come on down.

In the recesses of my memory bank, I do recall about a half an hour of preparation time generously given to us by our regular public school teacher. Far from being serious prep sessions, these were more like morale boosters or prep rallies. Toward the end of that session, I interrupted the teacher's inspirational pregame charge to ask a simple question: "What if we don't know the answer?"

"Not know the answer?"

The teacher looked at me with an odd, quizzical look, as if the possibility had never occurred to her.

"You can't say 'I don't know,'" she replied. "There is no place for that. Besides, you will lose points. If you don't know—guess! Always guess that the answer is B."

For some reason, the phrase *You can't say "I don't know"* stayed with me for a very long time. Never could I say "I don't know," I thought to myself, and many times I either feigned knowledge I didn't have or suffered a huge blow to my ego with the realization that I was violating my teacher's commandment. Since becoming a rabbi, however, I am far less afraid of that answer. "I don't know" demonstrates a humility that invites inquiry, then dialogue. "I don't know; what do you think?" has become a tried and true method to get students of all ages to think for themselves, a quality that no SAT can truly measure or appreciate.

Beware of religious practitioners who declare that they do know, that they possess the Truth. Absolute facts about either the immortal or mortal realms are terribly hard to come by.

Good scientists should also not be afraid of saying "I don't know" because they often really do not know. Astronomers tell us that there are over a hundred billion stars in our galaxy, perhaps a hundred billion in the universe. With the strongest telescope, we can only see a tiny percentage of the magnificent whole. For the most part, we don't even know the constitution of the universe. While researchers offer compelling evidence that the universe is filled with subatomic particles known as neutrinos, these possess no mass. Some physicists estimate that what is sometimes called "dark matter" composes between 90 to 99 percent of the galaxy. In fact, the Hebrew word for universe is *olam*, which comes from the root word meaning "that which is hidden away." The universe, indeed, is a mysterious place to inhabit.[22]

Mystery is just fine with one of the most brilliant scientists who ever lived: Albert Einstein. The man who at one time lived an observant Jewish life, keeping the prohibitions of the Sabbath and the kosher laws, once defined what he meant when he called himself religious:

> The most beautiful emotion we can experience is the mysterious. It is the fundamental emotion that stands at the cradle of all true art and science. He to whom this emotion is a stranger, who can no longer wonder and stand rapt in awe, is as good as dead, a snuffed-out candle. To sense that behind anything that can be experienced there is something their minds cannot grasp, whose beauty and sublimity reaches us only indirectly: this is religiousness.[23]

Feelings of awe presuppose a hunger for knowledge, a sense that we just don't know all there is to know. If we thought we did, both scientific and religious inquiry would cease. MIT astrophysicist Alan Lightman further explains:

> Scientists are happy, of course, when they find answers to questions. But scientists are also happy when they become stuck, when they discover interesting questions that they cannot answer. Because this is when their imaginations and creativity are set on fire. That is when the greatest progress occurs.
>
> One of the Holy Grails from physics is to find the so-called "theory of everything," the final theory that will encompass all the fundamental laws of nature. I, for one, hope that we never find that final theory. I hope there are always things that we

don't know—about the physical world as well as about ourselves. I believe in the creative power of the unknown. I believe in the exhilaration of standing on the boundary between the known and the unknown. I believe in the unanswered questions of children.[24]

So do I. I may not be able to even answer the existential questions of our kindergarten students, who often stun me with their depth. While students of all ages may occasionally say to me that they don't believe in religion, they believe in science, my answer is always that I believe in any path that will give us satisfactory answers to the mystery of why we are alive on this Earth and what we can and should do about that amazing event. Don't limit yourself to the world you are comfortable with, I tell them. Become uncomfortable in search of answers, in search of meaning.

That was why I found the following visit in my study last year so frustrating:

"Why haven't you taken your mother to her internist until now," I asked Bruce, a new member of our congregation who made an appointment with me to discuss his family's medical emergency.

"A few years ago, my mom remarried a man who was a Christian Scientist. That guy was really committed. He ran to the mother church in Boston regularly, tithed his income, and was a real believer. God is responsible for everything, blessing and suffering alike. He said it was fine to go to the dentist or fix a broken bone, but when it got really serious, he convinced my mother that doctors don't heal. The regeneration process can only be done by Christian Scientist spiritual healers."

"But your mom wasn't a member of the Christian Science Church, was she?"

"No, Rabbi, she is a Jew and a real believer in God. That's why she was so susceptible to his argument. He kept saying: 'It's the same God, Marge. Trust in God, just trust in God.' But, Rabbi," he said in a quivering voice, "she kept looking worse—gray, thin, drawn."

"How is she feeling now?"

"Terrible, declining every day. Each morning, I would call and tell her to go to the damn doctor; the next thing I know, those healers were back. For an hour or so she felt strong, and suddenly, she's back in bed. Finally, I wore her down. She told me to come see you, that you were wise and a real God-believer. You would be able to tell us all what to do."

Any religion that has as its basis a strong belief in a powerful God, like my faith Judaism or Christian Science, has the right to wonder why that powerful God should not be the ultimate healer. Why shouldn't we sit back and expect God to play that role? Jewish tradition regularly poses the question that if God has power over life and death, do we have any role in curing illness at all? Talmudic scholars began their inquiry with this early biblical legislation:

"When individuals quarrel and one strikes the other with a stone or a fist and the victim does not die but has to take to bed, if that victim then gets up and walks outdoors even upon a crutch, the assailant shall be prosecuted only for time lost, provided that he be thoroughly healed." (Exodus 21:18–19)

The last two words of the biblical quote that, literally translated, read "and he shall be completely healed" were seized upon by the Talmud as explicit permission for human beings to be involved in the healing process. Without this permission, human beings could be seen as interfering with the divine decree concerning the fate of a particular individual. The rabbis saw in this verse not only the divine intention that we be helped but that human beings use all their powers to make healing happen. Don't just sit back and wait—do something! In the Talmudic tractate Bava Kamma, Rabbi Ishmael said, "And he shall be healed." From this, it can be derived that authorization was granted by God to the healer or doctor to heal.

In another Talmudic source, Rabbi Yochanan once fell ill, and his friend, Rabbi Hanina, went in to visit him. Hanina said, "Give me your hand." He gave him his hand and he raised it. Why could not Rabbi Yochanan raise it himself? The Rabbi's reply: "The prisoner cannot free himself from jail." (Babylonian Talmud, Berachot 5b)

Perhaps because God cannot be everywhere, perhaps because we were created in the divine image, expected to utilize the knowledge we inherit and discover to improve the human condition, we are empowered by God, in the Talmud's view, to utilize both spiritual and scientific knowledge to help cure people's ills.

Why do some God-believers persist in the notion that God, and therefore we, have to go it alone? Christian Science is just another of those approaches that brooks no counterpoint, no penetration of wisdom from other disciplines. This faith, like some others, works to sequester its point of view, to stay in its corner like old boxers warily eyeing those in other corners, determined to stay on their own stools without direct encounter. Despite having no discernable hold on absolute truth, they persist in the belief that no meeting of the mind needs take place between science and religion, evolution and creationism, God and the Big Bang. Are universities the only places where we can find an interdisciplinary approach? Can't we apply the wisdom of one world to the other and emerge with a synthesis wiser than we can achieve if we stayed far away from each other?

To further illustrate the indisputable fact that science and religion once coexisted rather comfortably and can do so again, consider the work of Maimonides (1135–1204), a theologian and lawgiver who is so revered across the Jewish spectrum for his learning and his authority that on his tombstone in Tiberias is written "From Moses to Moses there is none like Moses."

Maimonides, also known as Rambam (an acronym for Rabbi Moshe ben Maimon), has written: "The science of stars...led us to acknowledge the form of the spheres, their number, their measure, the course they follow...and the orbit of every star and what its course is...This is an exceedingly glorious science."[25]

This towering rabbinic sage also proclaimed himself to be a proud Aristotelian whose God was not the omnipotent personal being who created the world and remains personally involved in the unfolding of human history. While for Aristotle the world is eternal and God the unmoved mover, the source and fountainhead of all motion, Maimonides differs somewhat in countering that God did in fact create the world. Yet Maimonides sounds much more like a physicist than a rabbi in positing the cosmological proof of the existence of God. Since every object in the world is moved by another, he reasons, there must be a force that starts the process of motion without being moved itself.[26]

Notice how useful Maimonides finds scientific principles in exploring God's role in fashioning the universe. As Maimonides understood and taught over eight hundred years ago, these worlds don't have to contradict but can help each other to gain renewed insight. While defending their rigorous critical methods, most scientists will admit that what passes for "truth" concerning some of the big questions, such as what is the origin of the world and how do all the species evolve, are only theories that will probably never be proven. Since firm scientific conclusions, thoroughly grounded in empirical rigor, seem remarkably elusive, scientists, like the rest of us, should approach our awesome universe with a bit of humility and good old spiritual wonder.

For example, people regularly opine that they don't believe in the Bible's view of the creation of the world; rather, they believe in the Big Bang. My question is, why do we have to pick between those approaches? Can't we believe in God's Big Bang?

As most researchers now believe, sometime around 13.7 billion years ago, our universe began as an infinitesimally small, incredibly hot, dense "something." The term often used for this something is *singularity*. How is this singularity defined? No one really knows. Where did it come from? No one knows. Why did it appear? Again, no one has a real clue.

Yet, as support for those who believe in the Big Bang, most scientists now believe that there was a beginning. This singularity appeared rather suddenly, apparently expanded, then cooled, turning into the universe as we know it today. Notice I didn't say anything about an actual "bang" because, apparently, no such explosion occurred. Think of a balloon that started to expand and never popped. In fact, our universe continues to expand to this very day, circling a beautiful star clustered together with several hundred billion other stars in our galaxy. At the same time, other galaxies are moving away from our own at speeds proportionate to their distance. This phenomenon is called Hubble's Law, named after astronomer Edwin Hubble (1889–1953), whose observations underscore the fact that the universe does in fact expand.

Many other scientists consistently attempt to make discoveries in support of the Big Bang theory. Radio astronomers Arno Penzias and Robert Wilson shared the 1978 Nobel Prize for Physics for discovering a cosmic radiation permeating the observable universe, providing supporting evidence that tremendous heat radiated at the very beginning of the Big Bang. This supports the view that both science and religion believe in a sudden beginning of the world as we know it.

Although we are learning more and more about what happened at the very beginning, more questions than answers remain. For example, an article in the *New York Times* posed the question: "How did the universe survive the Big Bang?"[27]

In other words, why did the universe not completely self-annihilate an instant after the Big Bang? Given the wide swings in temperature, how did Earth come to have an environment hospitable to the growth of life? Even the slightest variation of temperature would have made life impossible.

Just think what had to happen within seconds of the Big Bang. Nuclear forces were needed to bind proteins and neutrons into the nuclei of atoms. Electromagnetism was needed to keep atoms and molecules together, and gravity was needed to keep all the ingredients for life anchored to the surface of Earth.

It is almost impossible to rationally fathom how all this could have been in place so that the atmospheric conditions would be conducive for the evolution of species from the simple to the complex. Moreover, to read the unfolding of creation in the Bible's view is to find a potential cosmogony that, in lyrical and theological terms, is wholly consistent with the Big Bang theory.

Open the very first pages of Scripture. There you will see that God created the universe ex nihilo, from nothing, which, curiously enough, is also what scientists believe. The Bible then articulates the gradual unfolding of the universe as follows:

Day One: Creation of light and separation from darkness

Day Two: Separation of waters into sky and seas

Day Three: The gathering of water, which makes the creation of land possible

Day Four: The creation of sun, moon, and stars and the placing of them in orbit

Day Five: The appearance of sea and bird life

Day Six: The emergence of more sophisticated mammals, culminating in human beings

In creation, then, God sends forth energy in the form of sound (God speaks) and light, which generates heat. In the subsequent cooling process, the earth congealed, discrete bodies of water emerged, and the slow emergence of life began. Evolution of countless species developed over the course of time, millions of years, with a crescendo into humankind. The only way that the biblical story and the Darwinian theory seemingly part company is that the latter sees all this coming about through random mutation and natural selection. Thus, man appears on the world stage as a survivor.

In the Bible, man appears as a God-ordained miracle to be a partner in the ongoing work of creation. In the religious worldview, we don't have dominion over Earth because we are still standing, survival of the fittest. Rather, we have dominion because we were created in God's image, and, therefore, our power must be mitigated by moral responsibility for the stewardship of the Earth.

Of course, that is the biblical, religious vision. Billions of years after the creation of the world, brilliantly portrayed both by science and religion, millions of years after the first human being struggled to his feet, four thousand years after Abraham and Sarah answered the call to journey to a new land, we have still not begun to fulfill our human potential. The more we know in each discipline, the more we don't know. Is it possible that the resulting humility could and should impel us to reach out to each other in mutual need? In my view, then, science and religion need each other more than ever.

Religion needs science to understand how all that God put into place actually operates in the world, to understand the rational basis for what many still regard only with awe and wonder.

Religion needs science to help us come to realize our place in this galaxy and among so many others. Science must help us answer awesome questions: Does life exist elsewhere, and if so, can we form a relationship with other life? What do we do with the resulting knowledge that our galaxy is one of many?

Religion needs science to help us harvest stem cells so that we can live longer and in greater health and dignity.

Religion needs science to help us continue the sequencing of the human genome to know our genetic tendencies and help us, therefore, combat the diseases that destroy our bodies, our minds, and ultimately our lives.

At the same time, science needs religion to understand why the earth was created from nothingness.

Science needs religion to understand the purpose of evolution, the meaning of the survival of human beings as the dominant species on planet Earth.

Science needs religion to understand what are the ethical boundaries of scientific inquiry, when does too much knowledge make us less human than we ought to be, than God intends us to be?

Science needs religion to clearly state that God created us to use our minds in order to stretch the frontiers of scientific knowledge as far as they can go and to use that knowledge in service of all of God's children.

Science needs science to be science and God to be God.

Dr. Francis Collins, the director of the National Human Genome Institute, has said: "You'll never understand what it means to be a human being through naturalistic observation. You won't understand why you are here and what the meaning is. Science has no power to address these questions—and are they not the most important questions we ask ourselves?"[28]

Yes but only if we believe that we don't possess all the answers. Questioning presupposes wonder, being open to the knowledge still beyond our mortal grasp.

Seeking to fortify Bruce in his effort to help his mother, I posed one final rhetorical question: If God does not need us to carry on the work of creation and assist in the healing process, why were we put on this Earth to begin with? In my judgment, religion and science not only can meet, but they must meet in exquisite partnership because the survival and well-being of our planet may very well require all that and more.

As I said to Bruce, "That's what Christian Science means to me." That's what Jewish Science means to me as well.

# CHAPTER FIVE

# Red Ribbon Religion

**M**OLLY LOOKED TOTALLY DISTRAUGHT WHEN she took a seat in my office.

"How's Ben?" I asked, knowing that her six-year-old autistic son was the ostensible reason Molly wanted to see me.

"Rabbi, we're trying really hard. Ben is spending hours a day learning with a therapist. His teacher is excellent. She puts her face right up to his and forces him to make eye contact. At night, though, when I'm helping him put on his pajamas and brush his teeth, Ben looks like he's a million miles away."

Dabbing away her persistent tears, Molly continues, "Ben won't even look at me." Now her tears became sobs. "Tell me, tell me please, how did this happen to me? Why me? Before Ben was born, I really believed in God. But how can I now? Look what God has done to me and my beautiful son."

As she reached across the table for the ever-present tissue box, I noticed a familiar red string amongst a sea of silver bracelets.

"I see you're wearing a *bendel*," I commented.

"A what?"

"That red string bracelet you are wearing. The Yiddish word for it is bendel, meaning a ribbon."

"Oh, that." She smiled with a touch of embarrassment. "That's my protection. Lots of people I know have them."

That pricey piece of couture, worn on the left wrist by the likes of Madonna, Britney Spears, and Demi Moore, is typically cut from a larger piece that has been wrapped around the tomb of the biblical matriarch Rachel in Bethlehem. Rachel's tomb is located on the very route that Jewish exiles had to travel when their Temple was destroyed and many prominent citizens were exiled from their homes to Babylonia. Just as Rachel watched over those uprooted from their homes in ancient days, Kabbalists believe that her burial site is a key portal through which people today can access her powerful, protective energies. Some believe wearing a string that had touched the tombstone can transfer those powers and provide a vital defense against the Evil Eye.

Evil Eye, or Ayin Hara in Hebrew, is a name given to a type of curse created by people who glance at others with evil intent or ill feelings. As far back as the third century C.E., Rab, one of the great religious authorities among the Babylonian Jews, declared that ninety-nine out of one hundred deaths were caused by the Evil Eye. In many cultures, it was believed that water equated to life and dryness to death and that the true evil done by the Ayin Hara is that it caused living beings to literally "dry up," and that included babies, milking animals, young fruit trees, and nursing mothers. Some feared that the Evil Eye could bring on impotence by drying the semen.

Specific remedies for the Evil Eye are many and varied. Hand gestures are often used in Italy. In Muslim countries, parents will take a child who has returned home from an outing with strangers and burn a charcoal disc on the seeds of a plant, recite an ancient

Zoroastrian prayer against the Evil Eye, and direct the smoke against the child. In Mexico, unbroken eggs are passed over the face and body of the one allegedly afflicted with the Evil Eye, transferring three mouthfuls of water from the mouth of the person casting the Evil Eye to the mouth of the victim. Jews may spit three times, throw salt, or mouth "Kein nit Ayin Hara"—may there be no Evil Eye.

However, during key life-cycle moments such as marriage, childbirth, and death, such measures were not deemed sufficient. Elaborate rituals were developed, all designed to aggressively combat the Ayin Hara. Veiling the face of the bride was seen as a protective measure. The bride and groom wore a kittel, very similar to a white shroud, to deceive evil spirits into thinking they were going to a funeral instead of a wedding. Initially, even the breaking of a glass by a groom at a Jewish wedding seemed an attempt to frighten away demons with loud noise.

When a woman was about to give birth, many elaborate rouses were devised. Since the devil supposedly feared a closed circle in which he became entirely helpless, the woman was led around the table three times, making three complete circles. It was customary to spin a long thread for the Holy Ark in the synagogue and place it around the bed or abdomen of the woman. Mysterious powers were imbedded in the key to the synagogue because the key was an opener, suggesting the opening of the womb and the easing of the delivery. Sometimes female relatives ran into the synagogue, where they put their heads in the Holy Ark, wailing and praying for the pregnant woman. Often the same string wrapped around the belly of the woman was placed around the tombstone of a tzadik, or righteous man, for protection. Charms and amulets were placed above the head of the bed, under the pillow, over the door and windows, anywhere or everywhere.

When people were quite sick, the custom was to change their name or to add a name, confusing the Evil Eye or similar evil spirits into thinking that they had the wrong person. During a funeral procession, the group would bring the casket in front of the synagogue and stop, thus warning the evil spirits to stay away from the assembled. After the burial, a different route back from the cemetery was prescribed, thus confusing the forces of evil. The custom of covering mirrors in the home came about because of the fear that the soul projected in the mirror might be snatched away by the ghost of the deceased.

The reason for my spending so much time on these "practices" is to demonstrate how strongly so many people, both in ancient days and today, believe in the forces of good and evil. So my question is, why do many people have so much trouble believing in God but have no trouble putting their faith in charms, name changes, and red ribbons? Certainly, such beliefs cannot be attributed to today's stars of stage and screen who engage in such practices. Perhaps we might borrow a fashion idea or see a bad movie because one of the stars we like have promoted them, but I think few of us wish to get spiritual direction from such fountains of wisdom as Madonna or Britney.

Perhaps a better reason we grab hold of such remedies is that our view of the world is still quite childlike, so we are both comforted and convinced by the magic we think we can see more than the God that we cannot see. How thrilled we are when there's a puff of smoke and a magician makes the woman reappear from the ominous closet. If magic is defined as trying to make use of the mysterious for our purposes, many of us are in love with such magic. There is a power here, and we want to harness it! If we can just let the genie out of the bottle, we may hope against hope that it can grant us wishes and that we will be protected from the Evil Eye, evil spirits, and everything else we know to be lurking out there.

If we are honest with ourselves, protection from evil is what we would want from God as well. We want our God to be the ultimate magician. To the extent that we believe at all, in our minds, God is Superman sans cape who is supposed to arrive at the right moment and swoop us away from all harm, a Dorothy back to Kansas fantasy. Since our faith is often on shaky ground and because it is totally performance based, the first moment God doesn't show up, He's toast and so is our belief system. You can now better understand why someone wants to wear a protective amulet, a Jewish star, a Kabbalah ribbon: such devices never abandon us and act in our minds as a type of vaccine against destructive forces like the Evil Eye.

This leads me to the second reason we profess faith in Red Ribbon Religion. Since what we ultimately crave is protection against forces of evil, we hope and pray that Red Ribbon Religion is the altar we can bow at and find success. In fact, protection seems to be what God was offering when trying to sell Moses on the mission to return to Egypt and free the slaves. Moses was reluctant and pleaded that he was unworthy. God reassured him that He would be with Moses at all times and would demonstrate divine power by routing the Egyptians and taking the Israelite people away from them under His transcendent protection.

Because people are people and can often only believe what they see, God arms Moses with hocus-pocus, some divinely inspired tricks up his sleeves. When the Egyptians and Pharaoh's court do not believe that God is present, Moses simply throws down his stick that instantly turns into a snake. Puts his hand into his cloak and pulls it out—voilà!—a hand encrusted with snowy scales. Hand back in—they disappear! Magical powers are revealed to teach the Pharaoh and his court that God is the ultimate source of Moses's power. Yet, you see how easy it is to blur the lines. The casual observer might be more impressed with a purveyor of magic whom he can see than the supposed wizard behind the curtain or beyond the heavens. The people of Israel might have been thoroughly convinced that humans performed these feats because the Egyptian sorcerers and magicians were able to duplicate Moses's show.

So, in the Book of Exodus, Moses received one other source of protection, one other type of amulet to carry with him through the entire odyssey—the gift of the divine name. The four-letter name of God often pronounced Yahweh, which, according to the Torah, was not given to Abraham, Isaac, or Jacob, was now gifted to Moses. Perhaps Moses, too, believed that pronouncing the divine name would be a constant source of protection during those difficult days of negotiating with the Egyptian king or those long, lonely desert nights.

Suitably armed, Moses led the people out of Egypt. His next act of wonder clearly exceeded the competence of Egypt's magicians: With the Egyptian army in hot pursuit, the people of Israel came to the banks of the Sea of Reeds. Hopelessly trapped, the people probably began to panic. But Moses constantly called out: "Have no fear! Stand back and witness the deliverance that God will bring you today."

Then, according to the biblical text, came a real surprise:

> God then turns to Moses, saying: "Why do you cry out to me? Speak to the children of Israel and tell them to go forward! Moses, you must lift up your staff and hold your arm over the sea and split it, so the Israelites may march into the waters on dry ground...Let the Egyptians know that I am the Lord when I assert my authority against Pharaoh, his chariots and his horsemen"...Now, a pillar of cloud set up in front of them and formed a shield between them and the Egyptian army. This cloud amidst the darkness cast a spell upon the night, so that army could not come near the Israelites. Then the Egyptian army was swallowed up by the waters and the people of Israel were finally free. (Exodus 14:13–31)

Clearly, a series of miraculous events transpired to produce this remarkable redemption. As you can imagine, there have been hundreds of attempts to explain the parting of the sea and the pillar of clouds. Many scholars have attempted to offer seismological explanations, rational rejoinders to the incredible display of immanence described in the Bible. To the Israelites on the brink of death, this was a stunning event. They may not have known who was ultimately responsible, but Moses was the Houdini they saw who helped them escape the waters. The same magician made the Egyptians disappear, and that, too, was a pretty good trick.

In my role as rabbi, I have personally witnessed many forms of transference sent in my direction, none more common than projecting God's powers upon me. I have been credited with providing the world with a beautiful day and heard the plaintive plea of those who wanted the Yankees to win just one more playoff game. Often, though, it is in the more serious times of great pain and distress that people hope to tap into what they believe are my special powers. A man in my congregation, apparently in excellent health, was stricken with a heart attack while exercising. His heart had actually stopped; he was revived in the ER and was now unconscious.

His anxious family huddled around his bed. His oldest son, Todd, turned to me and with the terrified eyes of dread and expectation pleaded, "Rabbi, do something!"

Did Todd think that I was God's representative, God's messenger? Did he think that I personally possessed the power to lift the affliction of his father and free him from the bondage of the machines, the only thing keeping him alive?

Although I couldn't be sure what he thought, I knew that Todd was needy, so I put my arm around him and said the traditional prayer for healing, the Misheberach. Instantly, Todd felt better. "Dad heard that prayer," he shouted excitedly. "I felt a squeeze in my hand. He did feel it!"

Again, I wasn't sure who Todd was crediting with the help he felt he had received. It didn't seem to matter to Todd. Magic was taking place: His father seemingly had responded; whatever mysterious power existed out there was made manifest in that hospital room, and he was grateful.

Perhaps we can now better understand the power of the Hasidic Movement's Lubavitcher Rebbe. Why did people stand in line for hours to receive the Rebbe's blessings when many of them wouldn't be caught alive or even dead in a synagogue or church? Why brave the elements to seek a blessing if they never believe in blessings enough to go to services of worship?

My answer is that although the Rebbe himself always believed that whatever magical powers he possessed flowed directly from God, his followers and those standing in line most likely didn't actually believe that at all. In a certain sense, then, they are idolaters because they believe not in God but in the power of the Rebbe. It is spiritualized witchcraft that they hope against hope will work. If you need any further proof of that, note that over one thousand prayers continue to arrive each day by fax or online to the gravesite of this Rebbe, the very deceased Rebbe Menachem Mendel Schneerson.

"More people come here on a day-to-day basis than were able to come to the Rebbe during his lifetime," proclaims Rabbi Abba Refson, whose job it is to take these prayers from their technological source and bring the prayerful requests of those who are ill, down on their luck, or considering marriage to the eight-foot square patch of earth in front of the Rebbe's gravesite. These petitioners clearly believe that the Rebbe's powers remain, even though his physical life has ended.[29]

So what's the harm if people want to believe in Red Ribbon Religion? Just the crushing disappointment that will likely result when you realize, as did Dorothy, the scarecrow, the tin man, and the lion, that there is absolutely no wizard behind these curtains.

In magic, once we know how the magician did the trick, the power evaporates with the mystery. Since this type of faith is entirely performance driven, the Red Ribbon or the Rebbe is bound to disappoint in direct proportion to how much life disappoints. As we all know, inevitably, life does.

The second and even bigger problem with Red Ribbon Religion is that it is based on a false premise and can thus never properly deliver. Red Ribbon Religion says that all you have to do is put a ribbon on your wrist and do nothing else, and you will be protected forever and ever. A little girl holding her dolly or being hugged before bedtime by a parent has a right to such a fantasy of how the world works. We don't.

In a hospital room, Todd wanted to do everything he could to help his father. As I left, Todd said, with a look of inevitability, "My dad tells me all the time that I am his Kaddish'l. I'm the one who is supposed to say Kaddish for him."

Kaddish, which I briefly introduced in the second chapter, is a two-thousand-year-old prayer that was written at the same time as the New Testament's Lord's Prayer, which I recited for many years in my public school in Springfield, Massachusetts. After all these years, I still can remember the words:

> Our Father, who art in heaven,
> Hallowed be thy name.
> Thy kingdom come.
> Thy will be done,
> On earth as it is in heaven.

In the Lord's Prayer, Jesus is heralding the coming of the Kingdom of God on Earth, for which his followers must prepare.

In Judaism, God's reign over Earth is also both a proclamation and a goal:

Let the glory of God be extolled,

Let His great name be hallowed in the world whose creation He willed.

May His kingdom soon prevail, in our own day...

The goal of saying Kaddish, seemingly, is to consolidate God's majesty in the world. The worshipper seems to be saying that by proclaiming God's sovereignty, we help make it so. In earlier days, Kaddish was most likely not invoked at the end of every prayer service but was often recited at the end of a study session. Whenever a righteous man, a tzadik, died, his students and colleagues would gather at the home to study in honor of the deceased. Kaddish was often the concluding rite. The earliest connection between Kaddish and the dead were those concluding words to the study session held at the home. Over time, the connection between study and Kaddish was forgotten, as the Kaddish got established in the mind of the Jew as a daily ritual of mourning.

Who benefits from the recitation of this prayer? Do our words help to establish God's majesty over the Earth? The author of the prayer surely thought so. In any case, its words create great resonance in the minds of the mourners who often come to the synagogue, after someone dies or on the anniversary of a death, for the purpose of saying this prayer. Reciting these sentiments, that God is great and holy, at a time of personal loss is an act of courage. The Jew who says Kaddish declares a confidence in God that may have been sorely shaken in death.

Although the Kaddish seems to be a categorical declaration of faith, mourners usually come to it with very little bravado. For them, Kaddish is more often a plea for help and consolation: "God help me to see the light after this darkness, help me to go on, help me to see the goodness in your world."

The Kaddish thus becomes a protest against helplessness, a refutation of randomness. Things just don't happen to us; we are not witless victims of fate. There is much we can do to change our lives, to affect the destiny of the world, but only if the human and the divine realms are working in concert. The Kaddish requires a community, a quorum of ten in order to recite the prayer. There is a built-in human support system as well to help the grief-stricken and to proclaim that together we will wage the battle against cynicism and bitterness.

Kaddish can be beneficial for both humans and God. For our purposes in this chapter, though, can magical qualities be found in the Kaddish? By saying the Kaddish, for example, can we help the deceased for whom we say Kaddish in the world to come? Does the Kaddish'l, the person who says Kaddish for his or her loved one, have any power over what happens after his or her relative or friend dies?

The rabbis rejected such power, but the questions still linger, and tales to the contrary were told. The most famous story comes from a tenth-century liturgical commentary by a French scholar named Simhah ben Samuel from the town of Vitry, called the *Vitry Machzor*. In it, he recounts a tale concerning the second-century luminary Rabbi Akiba, who was walking in a cemetery and encountered a naked man shouldering an impossibly heavy burden of wood:

> "Why are you carrying such a load?" Akiba stopped to ask. "If you are in need of help, I will try to redeem you from your servitude."
>
> "Do not detain me, for the man you are looking at is a dead man. Every day I am sent out here to chop wood."
>
> "Tell me, my good man," Akiba inquired, "what was your work in this world before death?"
>
> "I was a tax collector, and I would favor the rich and torment the poor."
>
> "Have your superiors told you what, if anything, would help your situation?"

"For such a man, there can be no relief. I did hear something once, but, no, it would be impossible."

"What is it? Tell me."

"They said that if this poor man had a son and if that son stood before the congregation and said the words from Kaddish, 'May His Great Name be blessed,' they would release him from punishment. But I left my wife when she was pregnant, and I have no idea whether she had a boy or a girl. Anyway, who would teach this child Torah and how to say such a prayer?"

Akiba was deeply moved by the story and went to the town where they had lived. He asked about the man and the towns-people replied, "May his bones revert to dust." And his wife? "May her name be blotted from the earth."

"Did she have a son?"

"Yes, but he is a heathen and we didn't even bother to circumcise him."

Akiba was not deterred. He found the boy, circumcised him, and began to teach him. When the boy was greatly resistant, Akiba fasted and asked God for help. Finally, the Holy One opened the boy's heart, he became knowledgeable about Torah and prayer, and subsequently stood before the congregation and said the very words, "May His Great Name be blessed."

At that moment, his father was released from his eternal punishment.

Such beliefs never fully took hold in the Jewish community. Rabbis do not explicitly counsel congregants to say Kaddish for the purpose of effecting magic, of improving their loved ones' place in the world to come. Of course, we will never know for sure if saying Kaddish can help in these very ways. Yet even those who may use the Kaddish for like purposes, who may hope that their prayer will have some salutary benefit for their loved ones, are still different from those who stand back and wait for someone else to create magic, who slap on a bendel and hope that that will somehow avert evil and achieve good.

It seems to me that those who are reciting Kaddish are trying, even in a moment of great pain, to do something to help. They are not withdrawing from an activist role in the world, saying that there is nothing that I can do, so maybe someone else has the power that I don't have. They are not saying maybe I'll put my trust in the shaman or magician because I don't have enough faith in myself, my God, or my community to do anything to help. Rather, they are saying, "Damn it, I may not know if what I am doing will get results. But I was given a brain, a soul, and an ability to effect self-determination, and I'm going to give life a try again."

Isn't that what the Torah meant when God responded to Moses's plea that people should stand back and witness the salvation of God? God's answer is a type of rebuke to Moses: "Why do you cry out to me? Speak to the children of Israel and tell them to go forward." The Torah is saying that we must do this together. God and we need each other. True religion, the Torah seems to be saying, takes place when people and God meet their mutually interlocking and reinforcing obligations. The world is a messy place and needs maximum collective effort if results are to be achieved.

Perhaps the Torah is also saying that God's power must be activated by ours. We were not created to sit back and wait for Superman to appear or the Rebbe to do his thing or the Red Ribbon to deflect evil. We were meant to combat evil ourselves through divine inspiration and human goodness.

So, when Molly sat in front of me talking about her son Ben and their collective struggle with autism, I could have added some more hocus-pocus to the brew. Perhaps the new Kabbalah Energy Drink, the citrus carbonated beverage containing taurin, B vitamins, caffeine, and fused with Kabbalah water, to provide the help she needed.

What I did tell her was to keep the faith—Judaism—and to keep working. I told her that it was my firm belief that on the day when she looks into Ben's eyes and Ben looks straight back at her, she will absolutely see in the face of her son the face of God.

# CHAPTER SIX

# Where Was God during the Holocaust and 9/11?

SEPTEMBER 11, 2001, WAS AN absolutely beautiful day in New York City. Intense blue skies and dazzling bright sunshine greeted all who bothered to notice. I was on a bus heading to Riverside Church to speak at an interfaith housing conference. The speech that I never had a chance to deliver focused on the insecurity some New Yorkers felt as they tried to navigate the challenges of urban life. Little did I dream how tragically insecure all of us would feel in just minutes. On the bus, someone announced that a plane had struck one of the towers at the World Trade Center. How terrible for passengers and crew, I thought. What a tragic accident!

Stepping into the church, I confronted a room full of confused conference participants. Terrorism was now suspected. Frantic friends and relatives were trying to contact anyone they knew who had entered the twin towers. My assistant, Julie, got through to my cell phone and as calmly as she could told me to get to our Day School immediately. At the school, still spotty information was being shared as children sought reassurance. One seven-year-old sobbed inconsolably, certain that her father had perished in the flames. She didn't know at the time that her father worked in Queens, far from the carnage. Sadly, a few of these children would lose their fathers that day. Four men within our congregation died in that terrorist attack, and one of our night security guards, a fireman by day, got killed in the collapse of the Marriott Hotel adjacent to the World Trade Center.

Osama bin Laden's terrorists struck a devastating blow measured by loss of life, property, and confidence in our optimistic worldview. How could these hijackings and subsequent killings have happened? Where was God?

Of course, this is an incredibly compelling question, but hardly a new one. The "why" question has been asked throughout human history but never more than in the aftermath of the Nazi slaughter during World War II, a destruction so unspeakable as to be dubbed the Holocaust.

*Holocaust.* The word still sends chills down my spine. Nothing compares to this extraordinary genocide in all of human history. The sheer magnitude of the loss—six million Jews, at least three million other people—is impossible to fathom. On the Upper West Side of Manhattan, as in so many places around the world, the names of those destroyed by Nazi henchmen are read throughout the entire Holocaust Remembrance Day. Every year, we begin where we left off the year before, barely making a dent in the meticulously documented record of those brutally slaughtered.

Numbers are only part of this uniquely tragic story. The truth of the matter is that never before and never since has a government—in this case, one legally and democratically elected—sought to rid a whole continent and ultimately the entire world of every member of a particular people. This was intended to be the once and for all Final Solution to an insidious problem, and the Nazis were meticulous in pursuit of their bestial goal. Arguably, this obsession with Jews cost them their ultimate victory in World War II. Well before Hitler disastrously opened up the Eastern Front, thus diluting Nazi forces, he had already opened up the Jewish front and was never deterred from his single-minded goal of complete genocide.

As serious an indictment of humanity as the Holocaust represents, as much as the most basic assumptions about human nature were rendered naïve and baseless, nothing has caused us to question the existence, power, and relevance of God as has the Holocaust.

Ever since the enormity of the destruction began to hit home, whenever one poses the existential question "How could bad things happen to good people?" the Holocaust is invariably invoked in the same breath. Those who read Jewish texts, who open the prayer book, who attend a Seder and read that God once took the Israelites out of Egypt with a mighty hand and an outstretched arm have the right to ask where was God in our own day. Our ancestors in Egypt were slaves, to be sure, but they were not lambs to the slaughter, as Jews so often became under Nazi rule. These Jews needed God even more. So why didn't God dramatically reappear to redeem the Jewish people in modern times? If there ever was a time when a powerful God needed to manifest divine power, it was there in Europe at that cataclysmic moment. Yet tragedy on an unprecedented scale resulted. Why?

One possible answer is to declare that God was now dead or had never lived. Professor Richard Rubenstein said it most directly: "How can Jews believe in an omnipotent, beneficent God after Auschwitz? Traditional Jewish theology maintains that God is the ultimate, omnipotent actor in historical drama.... I fail to see how this position can be maintained without regarding Hitler and the SS as instruments of God's will."[30]

To Professor Eliezar Berkowitz, the promise inherent in past redemptions has been critically undermined through the Holocaust:

> Christianity promises redemption through a self-sacrificial act of God. The sacrifice was made, but all historic experience has gone to show that the promise has not been kept. Mankind has remained unredeemed. The question's relevance to Judaism I see is the fact among the untold abominations of human history, the murder of six million Jews in the heart of Christian Europe has been one of the most abominable. For me this fact proves that *that* God is indeed dead.[31]

Throughout religious history, however, there has been a stubborn insistence that God is far from dead, that the transcendent God was and remains imminent, powerful, and caring. Although texts like Isaiah 45:7 exist in Scriptures—"I form light and create darkness. I make peace and create evil; I, the Lord, do all these things"—the vast preponderance of theologians throughout the world do not feel that God is the direct cause or author of monstrous evil perpetuated upon humankind. Ultimately, they proclaim that human beings are responsible.

Turn to any of the prophets in the Hebrew Bible, and their message is remarkably clear and consistent: you know what you were supposed to do; you signed up for the covenant at Sinai together with those who actually stood there that day. However, you brazenly abrogated that sacred agreement. You worshipped other gods, became arrogant and immoral. You were deserving of punishment. Therefore, because you forsook God, God forsook you, albeit for a short time.

As the prophet Isaiah said:

> For a small moment have I forsaken thee; but with great compassion will I gather thee. In a little wrath I hid my face from thee for a

moment; but with everlasting kindness will I have compassion on thee. (Isaiah 54:7–8)

Hiding God's face could certainly result in incredible punishment, like the destruction of the Temple and the exile of key elements of Israelite society to Babylonia or Egypt. In traditional liturgy, Jews confess that "because of our sins, we were exiled from our land." In praying for the rebuilding of the Temple, in pleading for a second chance to show that we sinners have made atonement and thus are worthy to be returned to a redeemed Israel, we are emphatically saying that we, not God, are responsible.

Surely, no one could possibly say that following the Holocaust, isn't that true? Sadly, that is not the case. Rabbi David Ellenson, president of the Hebrew Union College-Jewish Institute of Religion, grew up in an Orthodox shul in Newport News, Virginia, and told me of a sermon in which his rabbi said that he could understand why the Jews of Western Europe were destroyed. They were not observant, totally assimilated, and could therefore be held responsible. What I don't understand, he intoned, is why the more pious Jews of Eastern Europe were also killed.

Ultra-Orthodox Satmar Rabbi Yoel Teitelbaum, fiercely anti-Zionist, proclaimed that God punished the Jews for having become Zionists: "The sectarians and heretics...demanded for themselves sovereignty and freedom before the appointed time, which is equivalent to hastening the redemption...It is not surprising therefore that we have witnessed this immense manifestation of God's anger...And during the destruction even the most saintly and pious people were killed on account of those who had sinned and caused others to sin...And the divine wrath was most fearsome and terrible to behold."[32]

To extend traditional biblical theodicy—that we are ultimately responsible for what happens to us—to the Holocaust seems illogical and obscene. European Jews in the twentieth century were certainly no more immoral than people in any other age. How could they possibly deserve a punishment of such magnitude? In every faith, in every century, people have challenged the assumption that evil perpetuated upon us was our own fault. Perhaps the most eloquent and prominent expositor of protest is the biblical Job.

Job is every man, any man. Purposely, we are not told where he was born or when. The book was written as a type of Greek tragedy, complete with prologue and epilogue. In the beginning of the book, we learn that Job was righteous and upright, a man who feared God and did no evil. He had seven sons, three daughters, and tremendous net worth.

The scene now switches to the heavens, where God is jousting with Satan, not yet the devil who will emerge in later Jewish and Christian sources but, rather, the obnoxious needler, the noodge, who tries to stick it to everyone, even God, every chance he gets.

Before Satan appears, God is in a jovial mood. Look at my boy Job down there, isn't he wonderful? He is so righteous and God-fearing.

Of course he is, snorts Satan, you have given him everything he could possibly ever want. Why don't we just put him to the test to see how righteous your Job really is?

Abruptly, everything is taken away from Job. His kids are slaughtered, natural disasters wipe out all his herds, and the man is afflicted with every skin ailment imaginable. He who once had it all now has lost it all. Immediately, Job's existential dilemma forces him to wrestle with the very same theodicy that all who have been stricken by life's woes confront. The calculation goes something like this: God is omnipotent and just; God certainly rewards the righteous and punishes the sinner; I am wholly righteous, yet I am being punished. Something in this picture does not compute.

Job, therefore, is beside himself with righteous indignation:

"Answer Thou me," Job thunders to the heavens. "How many are mine iniquities and sins? Make me to know my transgressions." (Job 13:22–3)

If I am in this state, Job here is saying, I had to do something to deserve it, but for the life of me, I don't know what that is. Help me, O God, help me.

His friends come to "comfort" Job, each offering his own rationalization. None, interestingly enough, questions the basic assumption of God's power and justice. Elifaz takes the position that there is no man without sin; therefore, Job is being disingenuous in claiming absolute rectitude. Bildad understands that Job thinks he is innocent, but since God is above reproach, Job is clearly not and deserves what happens to him. Tzofer thinks Job is utterly arrogant in forever proclaiming his innocence.

With friends like these, who needs enemies? Job is anything but appeased and demands a better answer. In my judgment, the questions posed by the Book of Job are far better than the answers he and we receive. But God does answer Job out of the whirlwind, thus reinforcing the power balance between the transcendent creator and man's creatureliness: "Where was thou when I laid the foundations of the earth?" (Job 38:4) In other words, you are in no position to ever understand my ways or the mysteries of how this planet operates. They will forever be inscrutable to you.

We do learn in one often forgotten line a crucial theological position of the book: "The Lord said to Elifaz the Temanite, 'My wrath is kindled against thee and against thy two friends since you have not spoken the right thing as my servant Job has.'" (Job 42:7) In other words, the author agrees with Job that there is no absolute correlation between the actions of individuals and the consequences that ensue. Job's suffering need not have an antecedent cause.

So why does Job suffer? God never does give him a good or straight answer, yet Job is mollified because he was able to "see" and "hear" God. Job is satisfied and ready to repent. How surprising and disconcerting, given the fury Job unleashed throughout the book. I like his earlier passion and cannot admire his docility here. Job is ready to slink away, happy that God has simply acknowledged his existence? What's that about?

This is not the divine-human relationship we signed up for. In Genesis 18, the God who was about to destroy the wicked cities of Sodom and Gomorrah comes down to tell Abraham about it. Does God need Abraham's permission? Hardly. God is testing Abraham to see how he will react to God's seemingly imperious ways. Abraham passes the test magnificently by refusing to skulk away or be passive, refusing to be God's cheerleader.

You're destroying those cities, Abraham is saying. What if there are innocent people there? Will Thou destroy the good together with the wicked? "Shall the judge of the entire earth not do justly?" (Genesis 18)

By refusing to back down, Abraham gets God to alter a previous resolution.

All right, God is saying, if you can find me ten righteous people in those cities, I will not destroy them.

Later, God makes another decision to destroy the Israelites themselves, who shockingly build a golden calf at the foot of Mount Sinai while Moses is receiving the Law at the top of the mountain. Moses cajoles God: For this, you brought the people out here to the desert? You're going to be the laughingstock amongst all the gods. Not fully successful with that line of reasoning, Moses now turns to pleading with God: All right, those people don't deserve to live, but you made a promise to their ancestors, to Abraham, Isaac, and Jacob, that they would be the ancestors of an eternal people armed with an everlasting covenant. For the sake of their righteousness, spare this people.

Forget for a moment whether these "dialogues" actually took place, whether these magnificent confrontations are factually true; clearly, the biblical paradigm does not encourage wimpishness and passivity. We are not to be simply grateful for our very existence in the face of perceived injustice. As people created in the image of God, we are both empowered and expected to do something about that injustice. Wiesel puts into the mouth of a tzadik his own magnificent protest:

> I have never questioned Your justice, Your mercy, though their ways have often confounded me. I have submitted to everything, accepted everything, not with resignation but with love and gratitude. I have accepted punishments, absurdities, slaughters. I have even let pass in the silence the death of one million children.
>
> But that's over...Do you hear? It's all over, I tell You. I cannot go on. If time and again You desert Your people, if this time again You permit the slaughterer to murder Your children and besmirch their allegiance to the covenant...know that You no longer deserve Your people's love and their passion to sanctify You...If this time again the survivors are massacred and their deaths held up to ridicule, know that I shall...fall to the ground, my forehead covered with ashes, and I shall weep as I have never wept in my life, and before dying I shall shout as no victim has ever shouted and know that each of my tears and each of my shouts will tarnish Your glory.[33]

So you see, what Judaism, indeed all Western religion, posits is truly a covenant with God, one in which we are not to remain silent but to open our hearts and our mouths in a full-throated relationship with God. This includes our right and duty to protest when gross injustice is taking place. As important and courageous as speaking up to God may be, it is not nearly enough. As I have already made clear in this book, I firmly believe in God but do not want to use God as a crutch or excuse, do not want to be a silent or uninvolved partner in the ongoing work of creating the best possible world.

God did not want that for us either. In the divine plan for creation, the very centerpiece was the human being, created to have dominion over all other living creatures. Clearly, God either had no interest in divine omnipotence or recognized the impossibility of remaining omnipotent in an evermore complicated world. Since we were created as potent beings with so much in our control, how could God possibly remain omnipotent? Even from the point of view of logic, such a position makes no sense.

In my judgment, God came down to Abraham before destroying Sodom and Gomorrah because God desperately needed a human partner to do together what neither could do alone. Moreover, God simply couldn't free the Israelite slaves from Egypt until Moses came along. God is no magician, and evil cannot be dissipated by a cloud of smoke and a dazzling array of magic. God needed not only the street "cred" of someone who at least lived in Egypt but needed the masterful diplomacy Moses and his brother Aaron brought in order to speak truth to power. If God ever could do it alone, since creation, God was no longer able to manage the world solo.

At Sinai, the covenant was established as a document not only of mutual responsibility but of mutual dependency. Here again, I'm not arguing that God and we are equal covenantal partners. But we do need each other. A number of rabbinic texts reinforce this point of view. In the Midrash, we read: "When humans do not do God's will, then (if we dare say such a thing) we weaken the Rock that begot thee, weaken the God who created thee. Conversely, when Israel does the will of the Holy One they enhance the power of the Almighty." (Pesikita De Rab Kahana 25:1)

The mystical text the Zohar is even clearer: "The Holy One once said: when Israel is worthy below, My power prevails in the universe; however, when Israel is found to be unworthy, she weakens My power above."

To come full circle, God fervently wishes for good to triumph over evil, descends from the heavens to the grimy, real world in order to work alongside human beings, constantly cajoles us to overcome apathy and indifference. However, because this is a partnership, God, too, can lose. In the Holocaust, God suffered many defeats. God simply couldn't triumph over the efficient Nazi obsession with killing Jews, which engaged many more people than the SS in their evil scheming. Hundreds of thousands of collaborators, Jew-haters, nationalists, profiteers, indifferent or scared people formed a formidable obstacle to the triumph of good.

God always needs us in the never-ending battle between righteousness and cruelty. For example, when the United States entered the war on the side of the allies, then the forces for good, both human and divine, were fortified for the fight. Throughout, God was there in the front lines, fighting and inspiring, rejoicing with every victory, crying with every defeat. Since both our strengths and our weaknesses reinforce each other, when we are fully human, working up to our full capacity to do all we can to defeat evil, then, and only then, can God be fully God. But make no mistake about this: In my judgment, God was present, not absent, during this horrible chapter in Jewish and human history.

So where was God in the Holocaust? God was in the Warsaw ghetto, fighting with the resisters who knew that they could not defeat the Nazis but who held out longer than many cities, thus diverting Nazi power from other places.

God was with the righteous gentiles who helped or hid Jews because "God wouldn't let me do otherwise" or "It was simply the right thing to do."

God was with every slaughtered person who refused to be defeated, who refused to give in to Nazi inhumanity, who tried to shield their children from death, who gave their parents the crust of bread they desperately needed for themselves in order to keep them alive.

God was with the people who kept themselves clean in the camps so they wouldn't succumb to infection. In *Legends of Our Time*, Wiesel wrote of the rebbe in Warsaw who stood erect before a group of SS. They amused themselves by making him suffer and by trying to humiliate him. But he refused to let himself be humiliated. As they cut off his beard and laughed hysterically, the rebbe stared directly into their eyes without flinching. This was his defiance, the expression of a man who would not be defeated, the expression of a man who "owes nothing to anyone, not even to God."[34]

That unbelievably courageous man owes nothing to God, but we do. For when we fail, when ultimately God and we fail together, I believe that God suffers along with us. The rabbis tell us that when the Temple was destroyed in Jerusalem and many of the Israelite people were exiled to Babylonian, the Shechina, the divine presence, wept. In Babylonia, the prophets who had been critical of the people's injustices now took on the role of bringing hope in God's name to the beleaguered and shell-shocked exiles. They fervently believed that if their listening audience did their part, God would respond in kind.

For thousands of years since then, God has often represented hope and even produced miracles at the most unlikely of times. Psychoanalyst Viktor Frankl wrote that he entered Auschwitz one night stripped of all his possessions and forever separated from his wife and children. He was left alone and proceeded to the next room, which turned out to contain showers. Throughout the ordeal, he had kept with him a copy of the manuscript he had been working on. It was the only thing left now that mattered. But he was being told that he would be killed if he tried to take anything into that chamber. Heartbroken, Frankl parted with the manuscript and followed his fellow victims.

After showering, he obtained a new suit of clothes once worn by a Jew who did not survive that selection and who was sent directly to the gas chambers. Sorrowful over the stranger's death and over the loss of his manuscript, Frankl slowly dressed in his new clothes, trying to accept the fact that he had now lost everything. As he dressed, however, he felt something in his shirt pocket. So, he reached in and found a piece of paper with writing on it and immediately began to cry. At that moment, when it seemed that life had lost all meaning, he found in those clothes what one man, now dead, had chosen to take with him in his walk into the gas chambers. It was a page from an old prayer book, and on it was written the words "Sh'ma Yisrael Adonai Eloheinu Adonai Echad"—Hear, O Israel, the Eternal is our God, the Eternal is one.

Even then, God was there. Frankl felt God's presence, and that hope kept him alive. In every situation, God needs us to acknowledge divine presence, our first responsibility in this partnership. Moreover, if we manifest the potential of being created in the image of God, in those actions, in that doing, we will find God. Because we are acting godly, God will seek us out as true partners.

It is easy to look at the enormity of the Holocaust and ask "Where was God?" Isn't that horrible chapter proof enough that God doesn't exist or certainly lacks power to help us?

As understandable as that reaction is, it also lets us off the hook. Sitting back and waiting for God to operate misses the whole point of our relationship and the self-imposed limitations on God's role. We either succeed or fail together.

On 9/11, God must have shared our outrage that human beings could carry out such a savage massacre. In my judgment, God once again stood and stands resolved to work with us to fight the common, ungodly foe. Moreover, thousands of years ago God promised that the covenant with us is eternal and that together we can sustain losses, but we will never suffer an ultimate defeat.

That promise ensures that although we may not win them all together, though we may suffer catastrophic losses as we did during the Holocaust and 9/11, we will ultimately prevail. We can make the world a better place, we can repair so much that was broken, we can even prevent another mass tragedy—but only if we act in partnership. In covenant. As God planned. Just as I heard it when I, too, stood at Sinai.

# CHAPTER SEVEN

## Affirming the God I Do Not Know

**T**HE SOUNDS OF AFFIRMATION VIRTUALLY shook the foundations of the synagogue. The sanctuary is full on these High Holidays, and the entire congregation is reciting the central words of faith with evident feeling and pronounced spirituality:

> Sh'ma Yisrael, Adonai Eloheinu, Adonai Echad
> Hear O Israel, the Lord is our God, the Lord is One.

Singing these words loudly and proudly, the congregation seems to be saying, "We embrace the truth: God is One. We know it. We feel it. We want to shout it out with such emotion as to leave no doubt about where we stand and what we believe." What an incredible, communal expression of shared faith.

A congregation of believers. A rabbi's dream. Even during the High Holidays, I wonder, is this really a room of believers? I am often so lost in the choreography of prayer, involved in shaping the experience, thinking about what's coming next, much like a coach so anticipating the next play that I do not focus on the answer to that provocative question. At this distance, however, I do wonder whether my congregation was truly praying and to whom. What, in fact, do they mean by God and that this God is One? Do they believe in God at all? A part of me feels an impish temptation to stop the service at some point and ask the assembled crowd whether they, in fact, feel God's presence. Do you really love God with your heart, soul, and mind, as the prayers say you do?

Is your God the supernatural persona who showers us with miracles, might, and mystery, the angry, nationalist God who punishes us for sin? Is God an imminent force in the universe who tries to inspire us to choose good over evil? Or is God a detached force who set the world in motion and then left us entirely to our own devices?

If I could stop the service for purpose of survey, I suspect that there would be a few people who would rather say, "Hear O Israel, I deny Eloheinu, I deny Echad."

A number of people would say that "Yes, God is One—but with explanation."

Many more would say, "Hear O Israel, I don't know Eloheinu, I don't know Echad!"

Why can't we enjoy theological certainty as so many of our kids seem to? In response to the question "How do you know there is a God?" some answers were offered a number of years ago in the publication *The American Rabbi:*

- There better be.
- There is a God because our Sunday school teacher told us and she knows stuff like that.

- Because it says so in the Bible and He wrote it, that's who.
- God loves everyone, even people you hate.
- I don't know who God is, we're not up to that yet (from a budding skeptic).
- God is whatever you think He is, but not a girl...
- God is very, very far away, but not so far away that He can't get here quick when the action starts (the Superman version).
- God is always around when you need help, but only with important things. Not your homework.[35]

Wouldn't you like to know that God is always present? We were once more certain, argues Charles Taylor in a recently published massive tome entitled *A Secular Age*. In pre-modern times, that deity demanded and deserved our worship, reverence, and love. In some cases, this devotion was itself seen as integral to human flourishing. Submerging our will to the divine mandate was part and parcel of the meaning of life. In fact, we were defined by faith, by who we worshipped, and what that God demanded of us.

No more. Today we live in an age of exclusive humanism, argues Taylor, an age featuring a rejection of a previously dominant Truth: a person can only be a proper moral agent imbedded in a larger spiritual hierarchy. Today, what bind us together are not timeless, transcendent laws but rather laws and ideas that we come to by common consensus and mutual self-interest. We would never have gotten here, Taylor claims, were it not for a profound shift of theology that for some reason he places in the seventeenth to eighteenth centuries. (Has he never heard of Maimonides?) No longer do we now think of God as the anthropomorphic being who continues to interact with us and compels obedience. God's role now is to endow us with reason so that we can grasp the orderliness of the universe and to carry out His plan—human flourishing—by ourselves. Taylor calls this theology "providential deism."

Having less God in our lives is the price we pay for liberation from a hierarchical theology in which we were clearly not on top of the social pyramid and in which our goals were subservient to God's.

Thus, modernity provokes a drift away from the Christian conception of God as a divine persona interacting with people and human history and toward the notion of God as architect of the universe operating by unchanging laws. This God can now be seen as no more than indifferent to our plight and eventually, because of lack of power and relevance, fades away to a state of nonexistence. In the nineteenth century, Taylor claims, unbelief came of age. Taylor does acknowledge that another result of this period of unbelief is a "wide sense of malaise at the disenchanted world, a sense of it as flat, empty, a multi-form search for something within, or beyond it, which could compensate for the meaning lost with transcendence; and this not only is a feature of that time, but as one which continues into ours." [36]

We haven't done so well or felt so fulfilled as the total masters of our fate. In fact, we hunger for that relationship not only with a transcendent realm but with a personal, caring God. We now wonder why we had to trade a state of being in which we were totally under God's control for a secular world where God has no role, and we find ourselves adrift with no transcendent relationships, goals, or purpose.

If we ever did want to live in a secular age, Taylor notwithstanding, I believe that we don't anymore.

Even if we are more prepared to posit the existence of God and in fact find it hard to imagine a world without a deity, this doesn't mean that our questions disappear. We are still not sure who God is and why so much evil exists. As I suggested at the beginning of the chapter, many will still find that we don't know Eloheinu, we don't know Echad. Of course, we want to know God. We want to have a fixed truth from which our lives make more sense and have more meaning. But we can't seem to acquire that knowledge and feeling to our complete satisfaction. The problem may lie with our outsized expectations.

God was Dan's constant companion. So it seemed because in every conversation, God was actively invoked.

"Dan," his friends would ask, "will you be at Tuesday night's card game?"

"God willing, God willing," he would answer constantly.

Or "How are you doing, Dan?"

"Thank God, thank God, really well."

Seemingly the only time he didn't invoke the divine name was when there was a reference to God's house or the activity of prayer. One day I said to him, "Hey, Dan, will I see you at services one of these days?" Then he didn't say, "God willing, God willing," because God certainly was willing, apparently more willing than Dan.

"Yes, of course, Rabbi," he would exult. The pew where he normally sat consistently remained empty.

One day he came to see me. Obviously distraught, Dan rambled on about how much government intervened in business, how an SEC investigation was pending any day.

Gentle probing produced a confession that his business had become too much of a personal piggy bank for the partners and that losses were buried deep in their books. That didn't stop Dan from railing against God's injustice:

"How could God do this to me? He is ruining me!"

I probably did not need to explain that the God of justice may very well be exacting some at that very moment. The Dan who had thanked God for everything was now blaming God for everything, forgetting that the God of love is also a God who expects human responsibility as part of the relationship. Our actions have consequences for our lives and for the way God relates to us.

Some authors have suggested that we don't fully understand God not only because we have blinders on where our actions are concerned, not only because we have changed the divine-human relationship, but also because God has changed over the course of time. In a widely read book, *God: A Biography,* Jack Miles asks us to see God as a literary character who grows, develops, changes, and even becomes more self-absorbed and less effective from the beginning of the Scriptures' story to the end. Whereas Miles himself questions whether the Bible purposefully intended literary development and dramatic change concerning the main character, he perseveres in his view that the Bible presents God as a protagonist in search of self-image.

God begins his career, Miles writes, with unlimited power and little self-knowledge. By the time we get to the last book of Scripture, God is filled with self-knowledge and little power. The God who created the world, the warrior who had won a great victory over Pharaoh, loses His sure footing as time goes on. The turning point for Miles is biblical Job's resistance to God's perceived injustice. While Job emerges victorious by standing firm in the battle, God "now knows that...he has a fiend susceptible side and that mankind's conscience can be finer than his."[37]

Having seen his self-image through the eyes of Job, God becomes dispirited, losing interest in his work and in self-growth. His only foe is himself. He too can't reconcile a good God with evil in the world. So, according to Miles, the God who started the world and its life with all the answers now has none. "He is trapped as Hamlet is trapped in himself."[38]

This book is a good read but is far from convincing and very far from uplifting. Coy in his ambivalence, does Miles still believe that presenting God as protagonist in search of self is built into the original intent of the text? Is Miles's reading of Scripture plausible?

It seems to be that a text that pays as close attention to development of character should have an author who is similarly focused on such development throughout. Virtually every non-Orthodox scholar roundly rejects the notion of a single author for the Bible. Although an editor or redactor had to bring all these sources together into the final product we have now, it is hardly likely that literary development of character would be high on the list of priorities.

More importantly, the Tanakh, or the Hebrew Bible, is quite explicit that God created the world and human beings precisely because He wished to enter into a relationship with them. The covenant was the key agreement, making clear that God and we would succeed or fail together. The goal, far more ambitious than God feeling good about Himself, was to reach the Promised Land, equipped with the Torah as constitution, to create the kind of world that God likely couldn't achieve alone. While the gods of the Greeks capriciously regarded people as their playthings, the Bible explicitly takes a strikingly different view: people are God's partners. Surely, God might have gone through life in as self-absorbed a mode as Miles contends, but chose not to. God's concerns for the Jewish people and all humankind are clearly in the text.

As the Book of Job is the watershed moment of God's downfall in Miles's view, I have to say that I totally disagree with his reading of that text. God remains fiery, defiant, and in control throughout. Job is the one who backs down. If anything, God and Job together defeat the worldview presented by the Book of Deuteronomy and given voice by the friends who come to comfort Job in his afflictions. This view is that since God is all powerful and just, if suffering befalls people, it is because they brought it on themselves. God responds to them, "You have not spoken of me, the thing that is right as my servant Job has." (Job 42:7) Job proclaims his innocence and insists that his suffering is not his fault. God supports and encourages him. Although the Book of Job does not give us the ultimate answer to the question

97

"Why do bad things happen to good people?" the book does contend that there is no necessary correlation between human suffering and human responsibility.

There is no evidence of Miles's view that biblical history has witnessed the tragic downfall of God the protagonist. All Western religions and millions of their adherents have all proclaimed that God is One, unified and unchanging. Why would we ever choose to reject that view in favor of God as Hamlet, strutting around the world stage muttering to Himself, mired in self-doubt, too paralyzed to act? Since the goal of religious life is to get to know who God is so we can know who we are and what we must do, we would have a really hard time falling in love and respecting a God who can't love and respect Himself.

Not always, however. The Bible argues that it is possible for human beings to help God with self-respect from time to time. Far from powerless, the God whom the Torah depicts on Mount Sinai is furious when the people, following their rescue from Egypt, build a golden calf. According to the Talmud, when Moses reaches the summit of Mount Sinai, God verbally assaults Moses and says, "Haven't I given you greatness because of the people of Israel? Now they have committed such a graven sin, what do I want from you? Get out! Let me alone that I might destroy this people."

Moses listens quietly and patiently and taking God's words to mean that if he left his divine partner alone, his people would be destroyed, but not if he stayed and negotiated on their behalf. So Moses holds his ground and cries out, "I will not let you go until you forgive and pardon them too." (Talmud Berachot 32a) Because of Moses's response, God rescinds the order of destruction. The dynamic of a strong, mutually interdependent relationship had new life and continues to this very day.

If God is growing and changing along with us, that does not mean that the relationship we have with God can't be updated. Recently, I received an e-mail whose original source failed to

announce itself. The e-mail suggested a more up-to-date relationship with God:

"Excuse me, sir."

"Is that you again, Moses?"

"I'm afraid it is, sir."

"What is it this time, Moses? More computer problems?"

"How did you guess?"

"I don't have to guess, Moses, remember?"

"Oh yes, I forgot."

"Tell me what do you want, Moses."

"But you already know, sir, remember?"

"Moses!"

"Sorry, sir."

"Well, go ahead, Moses, spit it out."

"Why the questions, sir? You know those ten 'things' you sent
me via e-mail?"

"You mean the Ten Commandments, Moses?"

"That's it. I was wondering if they are important."

"What do you mean 'If they are important?' Of course they're
important. Otherwise, I wouldn't send them to you."

"Well, sorry, sir, but I lost them..."

"What do you mean that you lost them? Are you trying to tell
me that you didn't save them, Moses?"

"No, sir, I forgot."

"You should always save things, Moses..."

"This computer stuff is just too much for me, sir. Can we go
back to those stone tablets? It was hard on my back taking them
down the mountain and reading them each day, but at least I
never lost them."

"We'll do it the new way, Moses. On the computer!"

"I was afraid you would say that, sir."

"Moses, what did I tell you to do if you messed up?"

"You told me to hold up the rat and point it toward the computer."

"Not the rat, the mouse, mouse! Did you do that?"

"No, I decided to try calling tech support first. After all, who knows more about this stuff than you? And I really like your hours...Wait a minute, sir, I am pointing the mouse and it seems to be working. Yes, a couple of the ten things have come back."

"Which ones are they, Moses?"

"Let me see. Thou shall not steal from any graven image. And thou shall not uncover thy neighbor's wife."

"Turn the computer off, Moses. I'm sending you another set of stone tablets."

Wouldn't it be nice if God had a website so we could verify divine revelation? Wouldn't we love to see God face to face on YouTube or, better still, on VideoChat? Our uncertainties would simply melt away. Although it is highly unlikely that we can have this kind of relationship with God, that doesn't mean that we don't want to try to figure out in every age how we can gain access to and insight from God.

In this regard, one of the most important developments in the post-Enlightenment period is the appearance of unprecedented theological diversity. Thinking variously about God didn't begin in modernity, but this trend exploded in the eighteenth and nineteenth centuries, particularly in Judaism and Christianity. My intention here is not to provide a thorough overview of these options, but I just want to contend that it is not so much that God is changing in relationship to human creations but that many people today are changing in relationship with God. When congregants now approach their clergy with the familiar phrase "I don't believe in God," we can confidently answer, "Well, tell me the concept of God you don't accept. I'll give you one you may very well embrace."

Those who have difficulties with the traditional biblical view of God as an omnipotent being who rewards and punishes us for our actions may turn to one of a number of tempting options on today's theological menu.

Some nontraditional options come from rationalists, thinkers who believe that understanding God must come from our own reasoning power, our intellect, the best resource we have to aspire to Truth. German theologian Hermann Cohen (1842–1918) rejects any human or sensual aspects to God. God for him is the highest ethical ideal that man can possibly attain, the eternal irreplaceable ground of the moral universe.

If Cohen's God is an idea, the very trustee of morality, then Mordechai Kaplan (1881–1983) holds on to the view that God, although not supernatural, is a force. Kaplan discerns a power in the universe that impels us to be the best, most moral person we can become. Man is so conditioned, Kaplan believes, to want to achieve true self-fulfillment, which he calls salvation. As that striving is self-evident, the human is eminently capable of getting in touch with a power that is within the universe and within each of us that helps us to achieve such salvation, our highest goal. God is not synonymous with conscience, argues Kaplan, but a force that is both independent and interdependent with human aspiration.

On the other end of the theological spectrum, we find existentialists, thinkers who believe that God can be found not through the use of reason or the mind but actually experienced by our total being. For famed Protestant theologian Søren Kierkegaard (1813–1855), God can only be discerned by suspending all inclinations toward and categories of rationality. Moreover, Kierkegaard never seeks to define God or even to try to articulate his God-concept. To do that would lead us back into the rationalist camp and away from the "absurd" faith that makes no rational sense but that we must hope to gain. To achieve this faith, we must aspire to "infinite resignation," the giving up of all previously held ideas of right and wrong in order to eventually achieve sublime faith. According to Kierkegaard, that is what biblical Abraham did in his willingness to bind and sacrifice his son Isaac. Abraham adopted a "teleological suspension of the ethical," the giving up of the socially acceptable rationalist view of what is the proper way to act in a situation and therefore acquired the faith that gave him back his son.

In his book *Fear and Trembling*, Kierkegaard writes:

> Although Abraham did not believe that God would require him to sacrifice his son, in his journey towards faith he was prepared to do so. On his walk on the mountain he reaches that stage of infinite resignation in which he is no longer tormented by his decisions. Then, he reaches the stage of faith in which he has his trust in God that makes absolutely no rational sense.[39]

Faith not only gives us a feeling of bliss and total connection of our being with the divine realm, but we give up nothing concrete to attain this state. That is how Kierkegaard can confidently declare that "only he who draws the knife gets Isaac."[40] Once again, Kierkegaard does not define this God or describe God's power or limitations. His focus is on us and what we will discover once we leave the rational behind, embrace the "absurd," and become a "knight of faith," living totally and blissfully in a relationship with God.

The final thinker I will present in this brief survey is Martin Buber (1878–1956), who also believes that we can't define God or discover God by rational means. God can only be "met." What Buber means by this is we can never know in absolute terms God's power, properties, or qualities. So infinitely above us, God can never become known in this way. We can only know what we feel when we are in a relationship with God. In fact, there is no objective, rational truth in Buber's mind. Everything we know comes to us when we enter into a relationship with everything around us. In Buber's thought, there are two types of relationships: the I–It encounter and the I–Thou. The I–It encounter happens 99.9 percent of the time. These are the everyday relationships in which we relate to others for our own purposes: our friends when we want to make plans, our teachers when we want to learn from them, our computers when we want to respond to e-mails. Most of our encounters with the people we love the most are in the I–It mode. Then, we are fully aware of the fact that we need something from the other: to discuss the day, to ask our kids if they have homework, to argue over who will set the table. The I–It relationships are not bad; they are simply utilitarian. Without them, we'd have no everyday communication or commerce.

Every once in a while, however, you are in relationship with something or someone in which you totally suspend the awareness of the moment. You are totally present. Your friend in school has a crisis, and for that moment, you are enveloped in that person's pain. You come home and your beloved dog, who has waited for you all day, jumps into your arms and licks your face. For that moment, nobody and nothing else matters. You are totally engrossed by the selfless love you feel for your pet. Then you are in the I–Thou moment. However, the moment you become aware of what you're doing, the moment the wetness of his tongue begins to annoy you to say, "All right, enough already," you have returned to the I–It encounter with the same dog. You can be in the I–Thou moment with an inanimate object, a beloved tree on your property, a sunset that leaves you mesmerized. But you can't stay there very long.

Buber believed that every time you are in the I–Thou, God is present as the Eternal Thou. Such an encounter can happen in a formal setting like a synagogue or church but can also take place any time or anywhere when you are totally enveloped in that relationship. Although Buber mostly thinks of these "meetings" as individualistic, there are times like at Mount Sinai, when a whole people can have an I–Thou relationship with God.

In fact, Buber believes that God is always available to us as an Eternal Thou, always prepared to be met. The problem is that you and I rarely stop running long enough, refuse to put down our BlackBerrys, and tend to see the world and other people as objects for our personal pleasure and advancement that we rarely lose ourselves totally to precious people and experiences. However, if we are able to find a way to have such "meetings," we will discover a great deal about ourselves, our God, and the relationship between us.

I could have gone further back in history and discussed Maimonides' neo-Aristotelian concept of God as the one who set all processes of creation in motion, who is the cause of all existence but lacks human attributes, and is much less of a personal God than the Bible describes, or Baruch Spinoza's pantheism that got him excommunicated by seventeenth-century traditional Jewish authorities but who would be right at home in the wide-ranging theological conversations of today. The point of introducing you to these thinkers is not to provide a course on modern theology but to simply reassure you that there's a place at the table and certainly a place at most synagogues and churches for your views. Don't think that you are doing something wrong, inauthentic, or blasphemous if you hold a different view of God. Whatever you now believe, chances are that there is a deeply respected, accepted, and authentic thinker who has already articulated something close to your precise beliefs.

Another important reason for providing this spectrum of beliefs is that virtually all of us, and that definitely includes almost all clergy I know, have struggled with what they believe in, often rejecting God-belief for a while, embracing and discarding several God-concepts in their lives, and in many cases still find themselves on a faith journey in order to formulate their concrete beliefs. If they can do this, so can you and so should you.

In a marvelous sermon printed in *The American Rabbi,* the brilliant Protestant minister David Rankin discussed his long trip back to God:

When I was a child I dwelled in God...When I played in the grass, I was rolling on the skin of God...When I gazed up at the stars, I was staring into the eyes of God...How should I describe the total feeling? It was inner warmth, like being held. It was gracious acceptance...

Then, I was sent to church...

I was told about a couple in a garden who messed up the whole creation.

I was told about the human body, which was born in sin and disgusting to behold.

I was told about a fearful, jealous God that destroyed the children of the enemies.

I was told about a victim on a cross, who would save a few from the fires of hell.

Yes...It was taught with a cordial smile, with milk and cookies, and a gold star for quoting the textbook properly...

They put God in a little box, wrapped it with their fears, tied it with their guilt and gave it to little children...

At the age of fourteen, I walked out of the church...

Luckily, growing up is forever and ever.

Gradually, I began to unravel the problem. While rejecting the gods of orthodox churches I unwittingly accepted their definition. When asked if I believed in God, I flatly responded, "No," but it was really a reference to the God of the Sunday school. Why did I retain that image?...

Then, too, I discovered I was not God...

Reluctantly...I was forced to confess: I am mortal...I am limited...I am dependent...I am nourished and sustained by forces and energies beyond myself...So when I abandoned the angry, tyrannical God, while admitting to my own dependency, I knew it was time for a major reconstruction...

I am still growing up with God...

Oddly, I am also growing back to God. No...it is not the innocence of childhood, but it is a familiar feeling...Gone are the images of a cruel despot. Gone are the negatives of adolescence...

At the age of fifty-two, from the study, I look out into the woods. Everything that exists is bathed in God...

In the smiles of men and women I see God. And in the sun's rays and the moon face I see God. And in my own inner self I see God...Look closely...Feel deeply...The world is charged with a grandeur of God.[41]

Rankin's journey resonates with my own. Unlike Rankin, I did not dramatically walk out of the synagogue. But it is true that through most of my high school days, I prayed regularly and was extremely active in the synagogue, Hebrew high school, and youth group. However, in the first couple of years of college, I just drifted, not really committed to any Jewish organization, not sure anymore what I believed or where I belonged. My year at the Hebrew University in Jerusalem was my attempt to figure out my relationship both with the State of Israel—which was savaged on campus at Columbia, often by Jews, as a colonialist and imperialist nation—and with my Jewish identity.

One Shabbat, I drifted into a Reconstructionalist congregation in Jerusalem, subconsciously at least, looking for a God-concept that would be easier for me so I didn't have to confront the God who does so much good but was also capable of engineering the deaths of Egyptian firstborn babies so the Israelite slaves could go free. In that synagogue, I was enraptured with the person of Kaplan, the founder of Reconstructionalism, wearing tallit and kippah, swaying to prayer as fervently as any Orthodox Jew.

I was mesmerized first because I was reminded of my grandfather and the men we sat with in synagogue when I was a boy. On another level, I wondered how a man who does not believe in a supernatural God, a being who answers prayers, could pray so fervently. Was he praying to get in touch with a force that makes for human salvation? Was he praying for community well-being? Was this just tradition for him? As a young college student, I didn't have the courage to approach him to ask that question. At a distance, I was fascinated but ultimately unconvinced. I needed to find my way back to the God who had done so much for me.

Using Abraham and Moses as paradigms, I knew I could argue with God. In fact, He would welcome heartfelt battle, and in my college-age egoism, I imagined God waiting patiently for me to return to the relationship, as heartbroken parents often wait for their estranged kids to return to them. In Israel, I began to think about applying to rabbinical school not so much because I knew I wanted to become a rabbi, but because I wanted to become a Jew and mostly to find a way back to God.

In my first year of rabbinical school in New York, I took a Jewish theology course with the brilliant and penetrating professor Eugene B. Borowitz. He put modern Jewish theology in sociological context, then introduced thinkers on both the rationalist and existentialist sides of the spectrum, like Cohen, Kaplan, Buber, and Heschel. Borowitz analyzed these men soberly, pointing out the wisdom they bring to the table as well as their shortcomings. The more I read, the more resolved I became to seek a personal relationship with the God who truly cares about His creations.

Borowitz's own concept, covenantal theology, was a godsend to me. Committed to Reform Judaism, Borowitz insisted that autonomy, the freedom to choose one's own course, is a given for the modern searcher. We should never surrender ourselves totally to any ideology or concept, including God. But as part of the covenant, it is selfish and irresponsible to separate ourselves from this historic experience and mission of the Jewish people. So, autonomy must be asserted in the context of responsibility for the history, faith, and fate of the Jewish people. Moreover, our universality, our desire to be there for human beings regardless of race or religion and our desire to join others in tikkun olam, the repair of the world, flows from this strong base of particularity. One cannot serve others well unless one has a strong and secure identity and source of values from which heartfelt positions emerge.

While still burdened with questions, I found myself in a deeply satisfying covenantal bond. If you think about it, every relationship that truly matters—with a parent, a mate, a child, a sibling— is complicated. You often feel like you are not on the same page. But you love them so deeply that you can't imagine the other not being a part of your life. That's the connection I was now able to make. Finally, I once again had a relationship with God to help me define who I was and what I had to do.

In rabbinical school, I came to realize what I'm sharing with you now: there are so many options, so many opportunities to find a God-concept that appeals to the intellect or the soul, so many ways to believe in God and to stand together, proclaiming the oneness of God. I felt grateful for this freedom because it allowed me to find my way back to the place I once stood and the ground that I had always wanted to reclaim.

You should know, however, that not everyone loves so many theological options. Sandy, a woman studying to convert to Judaism, came to me in tears. "I really appreciate the freedom that liberal Judaism offers us to figure out what we believe. I really do. When I was a Catholic girl taking Communion, I used to resent being told that I was ingesting Christ. It was as if it was all shoved down my throat. Now I feel free of religion choking me—but almost too free, if you know what I mean. All these concepts, all these options, it is overwhelming. I thought I'd feel really good about myself, but I guess I really don't. I just feel confused and inadequate."

Sandy reminded me that modernity, with its unprecedented freedom, is not an unalloyed blessing.

In fact, modernity can make you miserable and theological options can leave you less inspired and more confused. Still, I come down firmly on the side of wanting people to learn more about others' struggles and conclusions in relationship to God. They need permission to wander, sometimes far afield, in order to return more sure and more resolved, more determined to develop this important relationship in their life. The conclusion I have come to, that which I have learned on my own journey, is that it matters less what precisely your God-concept is. What really matters is that your relationship to God has to make a difference in your life and in your world. God has to matter.

Steinberg writes:

> God is the force that resolves the terrible contradiction, the intolerable tension of life. And for this purpose it does not especially matter how we conceive God. I have been a great zealot for a mature idea of God. I have urged again and again that we think through our theology, not limping along on a child's notion of God as an old man in the sky. But for my immediate purpose, all this is irrelevant. What is relevant is this: that so soon as a man believes in God, so soon as he wills to believe in Him, the terrible strain is eased; nay it disappears...Because a new and higher purpose is introduced in life, the purpose of doing the will of God.[42]

Belief in God permits us then to believe in ourselves and to believe that life does not consist of just individuals trying to climb up the ladder of success. Life, indeed, has meaning, a deeper purpose. We truly are not alone.

Everyone who stands in the congregation proclaiming that God is One senses how important that declaration is. At that moment, they're not focused on the literal meaning of the words or even precisely what they believe about God. They are standing together in solidarity, in covenant, feeling each other's friendship, longings, pain, and struggles.

They are saying to their God, whatever their concept is, okay, sometimes I have questions about You, but You must have questions about us. Sometimes, I do wonder where You are when I need You, and You must be saying the same thing about me. But we're in this together against common enemies—all those who worship idols, things that have little ultimate value and which conspire to make this world godless. Our covenant with You, God, is eternal. Therefore, we can outlast our enemies if, and only if, we stand together.

At that sacred moment of prayer, we are resolving to do exactly that: stand together against the common foe.

So it's no more:

Hear O Israel, I deny Eloheinu, I deny Echad.

It's no more:

I don't know Eloheinu. I don't know Echad.

We are saying:

*Hear O Israel, I know Eloheinu, I know Echad, that God is One.*

That knowledge can make all the difference in your life so you can go out into the world and make a difference in someone else's life.

Then God will have fewer doubts about us as well.

# CHAPTER EIGHT

◦

# The Arrogance of
# Self-Sufficiency

**H**AVE YOU HEARD *THE SECRET?* Hard to imagine that you haven't because between the book and the DVD, it has sold over four million copies and qualifies as one of the bestselling self-help books of all time.

Before you hyperventilate with excitement, however, I must burst your bubble. Like many secrets, this one never should have gotten out. Like many secrets, this one is utter nonsense until someone believes it. Then, it is downright dangerous.

Author Rhonda Byrne even has the chutzpah to elevate her pabulum to the realm of law. Her secret is the "law of attraction," which states that if people simply envision what they want—like great wealth or total health—and as long as they keep out of mind any negative images that could undermine their goals, they are as good as done. That's all you have to do to get everything you ever wanted or think you deserve!

How is that possible? Byrne here posits the theology of narcissism. In the book, she presents a man named John Hazelton, who articulates what he calls quantum cosmology, that we are the source of the universe, have ultimate authority, and can therefore achieve anything. Jack Canfield, who conceived the remarkable *Chicken Soup* series and who adds his wisdom to Byrne's book, says that *The Secret* brought him a 4.5-million dollar mansion, a "wife to die for," and vacations all over the world. Now, Jack, might these rewards have materialized because of the gazillion *Chicken Soup* books sold? Let's not let common sense intrude. Rhonda Byrne is on a roll: "You are the master of the universe...You are the perfection of life."[43] As the master of the universe, you cannot "catch anything unless you think you can, and thinking you can is inviting it to you with your thought. You are also inviting illness, if you are listening to people talking about their illness..."[44]

So, the goal of life here is to stay away from every other person in the world who might bring a negative thought into your orbit. That means stay by yourself and think the good thoughts, which will get you the McMansion, trophy mates, and the disease-free existence you have always wanted.

How do bad things happen to good people? Clearly, they defy the "law of attraction" by attracting bad things to themselves. Anything that goes wrong is *your fault*. Help me, Rhonda: Should I tell the family who lost their child to an inoperable brain tumor that they just didn't follow the law of attraction, that negative vibes killed their son?

Welcome to the Church of Wholly Selfishness, where you are the God who cares for absolutely no one else. You are alone! Don't come near anyone else or their vibe may bring you down. If this is what the ladder of success is supposed to look like today, let me down.

In my mind, you have just read a description of a world without God. No expectations, no standards, no responsibilities, no caring. That's not a dream; it's a nightmare. Fortunately, you can wake up from your nightmare because there is a more compelling truth in the world, and it is no secret. In fact, it's as old as creation itself and is taught in the very first chapter in the Bible. *You are not alone!*

The world does not revolve around you; therefore, you don't have to do it all yourself. In fact, you fulfill your true potential only when you care for and are cared for by those beyond yourself.

Moses learned this truth in his own life. As the adopted son of the Egyptian pharaoh, he had everything a narcissist would want. Perhaps an autographed copy of *The Secret*, for all we know. Although the people he was born into were suffering all the degradations of slavery, Moses was oblivious, responsible for nothing and no one.

What had been a distant abstraction clearly shocked him when he personally witnessed the suffering of his brethren. When an Egyptian overlord whipped an Israelite slave, Moses's innate sense of justice came to the fore. He simply could not tolerate what he was seeing. So he struck down the tormentor, then fled for his life into the serene desert of Midian.

Far from the long arm of Egyptian justice, he settled into a private, nomadic life, marrying the daughter of a Midian priest named Jethro and taking a job as a shepherd for his father-in-law's flocks. Far from home, Moses was never alone. One day, God appeared to him within a thorn bush. This was a wondrous sight impossible to ignore because this bush continued to burn without additional kindling or stoking. Astonished, Moses stopped to gaze at the phenomenon of the bush that would not be consumed.

God, in turn, noticed his sense of wonder. Then, and only then, did Moses hear the divine call from within the bush. "Moses. Moses." And Moses answered, "Hineni. Here I am."

Even traditional biblical commentators questioned how God actually communicates with us. So, in a beautiful Midrash, a rabbinical commentary based on a biblical text, God frets about how Moses would receive the awesome power of the almighty: "If I reveal myself in a loud voice, I will terrify him. If in a soft voice, he will think lightly of prophecy." So, God was revealed in the voice of Moses's father. Here, the rabbis teach that God can come to us not as some thunderous sound from above but through intimate voices we carry around in our subconscious of people we cherish.

In awesome events big and small, we can sense the presence of God and know we are not alone. As my own daughter Maya said in her Bat Mitzvah speech on September 8, 2007, "Miracles have to be believed to be seen." Clearly, Moses was spiritually attuned to be open to the presence of God. A hundred other people might walk nonchalantly past a bush; only Moses took notice. The Bible indicates that God had more in mind than a mystical experience in the desert. God has expectations of us humans, and Moses, who still seethed from the injustices he saw, was His chosen partner. Moses didn't react well to that revelation, did not believe he was worthy of the prophetic call:

"Who am I to go to the Pharaoh?" he bellowed. "I never have been a man of words, for I am slow of speech and tongue. Not only that but they'll never believe that the Lord has appeared to me."

Humility made him reluctant to realize he must speak truth to power, return to Egypt, and be God's prophet, God's partner. The prophet has no choice. Moses knew in the very depth of his being that there was something he had to do. This was his life's work, the reason that he received the gift of life. As God's chosen messenger, he dared not demur. At least in the recesses of his being, Moses had to be grateful that even in the desert, God had not forgotten him. Moses was not alone, and that reassurance must have meant much to him.

That reassurance meant everything to me as well. Today, I seek God for myself and hundreds of others regularly as the rabbi of a large New York congregation. The last words of the Friday evening service, coming from the Adon Olam (The Eternal God), read: "God is with me, I have no fear." That's our collective aspiration, but it is rarely my certainty. I, too, regularly question, yet at least twice in my pre-rabbinic life did I believe to the core of my being that God had directly entered my life.

When I was growing up, I had a minor case of cerebral palsy. Believe me, in the world of CP, I've always considered myself remarkably blessed, but when I was an infant, a prominent orthopedic surgeon predicated that I would never walk and I could very well suffer mental impairment. That horrific scenario never came to pass, but I did walk with a pronounced limp and had to teach myself to walk heel-toe, heel-toe. My athletic skills suffered as a result. Try as I might, I didn't have the strength to drag my body across the playground's jungle gym bars.

Thankfully, I could walk, run slowly, and swing a baseball bat with far too little power. However, when I was twelve years old, I experienced an anatomical miracle that I never understood. Up to that point in my life, my right foot was always significantly larger than my left, usually close to three sizes worth. Either I had to special-order shoes or buy two pairs. Remarkably, my feet that year grew to within a half size of each other and now I rarely notice the difference. What's that about?

Perhaps because of my CP, my social calendar was rarely full. I would often sit in my backyard and play a dice baseball game that I had invented, announcing every dramatic inning with a booming voice that was God's gift. Sometimes, I would take a break from the ballgame and sit on a long swing underneath the maple tree and talk to God. Whether I was in the synagogue or in my backyard, I took my relationship with God in stride. God didn't have to prove anything to me, and I would usually talk one-on-one, never expecting or hearing any reply. One time, though, everything was different. God didn't appear to me in a physical manifestation or a burning bush; God didn't speak at all. What I did feel was a jolt that surged through me like a massive wind that hurls you backward. It didn't last long, but the surge had a remarkable effect on me. Calm prevailed, replacing a disquieting loneliness. That day, I knew I was not alone.

The second occurrence took place during my freshman year at Columbia University in New York City. For a time, I battled depression, which seemed to block my full comprehension of all I needed to do academically in an incredibly demanding core curriculum. Every day seemed like a Herculean struggle just to cope. More than once, I wondered whether if it was worth it. One night, while lying in bed, I felt God's presence again, a feeling even less gentle, more persistent. Once again, I knew that I was not alone. What God communicated to me that night was that there was a reason for me to keep going, something I must do.

Knowing that I was not alone meant everything to me. I felt that God's communication with me was a type of calling to which I had to respond. There was something I had to do, which was to bring the message of God's presence to others, to do for God what God could not do alone.

Connecting to others became my oxygen, my purpose in life. As a rabbi, I know how desperately people need to feel a part of something larger than themselves. It is often because they no longer feel protected by the key people in core institutions of their lives. It will not help them to learn *The Secret,* which makes matters worse by counseling us to stay away from each other lest we become infected with negative vibes and miss out on all of life's goodies. In my experience, such narcissism doesn't make us any happier, just more lonely.

Such obsession with self can serve as a metaphor for our times. Gone are the days when families lived in two-story tenements in the same neighborhood, an era that was beautifully captured by nostalgic filmmakers Barry Levinson, Woody Allen, and Neil Simon. Families made up of mom, pop, three children, and a dog named Skippy seem almost like quaint memories and are experienced by less than half of the population. More often than not, our families are wounded, and their members feel increasingly on their own. When you ask parents if their kids live near them, it's not atypical to hear that one lives in California, another in London, and a third is at home until she can earn enough money so she can leave the family home for good.

From the time they let go of their parents' finger and take those first steps, kids try really hard to be on their own. Liberation from rules, curfews, and moralizing lectures is the goal of freedom-loving children everywhere. Years ago, Dr. Anthony Wolf wrote a book called *Get Out of My Life, But First Could You Drive Me and Cheryl to the Mall?* Today, they don't have to go anywhere. All they have to do is enter their rooms, slam the doors, sit in front of their computers, and lose themselves in their favorite websites. Kids now spend far less time reading *Teen, People,* and *Us* and more time on MySpace and VideoChat. Notice how these sites are labeled—MySpace is enticing precisely because it involves me and not us. Kids love Facebook because they get to look in on people's lives. They can be voyeurs without really communicating. Instant messages are sound bites, not discussions. Dot.com entrepreneurs build three-million-person strong "communities," and you know how close they can be. *Newsweek* concludes its article "The New Wisdom of the Web" with these words: "The web is where we live, and is certainly the address kids most easily relate to."[45]

Of course, if we are honest with ourselves, parents do the exact same thing. Literally, billions of e-mails are sent every week and are fast supplanting the phone as the medium of choice. We all get e-mails sent at 4 a.m. Why are people sending e-mails at that outrageous hour? Because the senders really do not want to talk.

They may want an answer to their question but certainly do not seek connection to others. That's one of the secrets today. It's not so much the law of attraction; it's the law of opposition—stay away from me, from any meaningful contact.

No wonder that people are sending out and receiving more communication than ever before and are often lonelier than ever before. Profits certainly grow online. Friendships rarely do.

Kids in fact spend more and more time living on the web, totally in control of how they present themselves yet lacking in maturity to know the implications. This is increasingly dangerous because, as the title of Thomas Friedman's op-ed in the *New York Times* puts it, "The Whole World Is Watching." Anything you say online is saved forever as a digital fingerprint and could come back to haunt you. In Friedman's words: "Our generation got to screw up and none of those screw-ups appeared on our first job resumes, which we got to write. For this generation, much of what they say, do, or write will be preserved online forever. Before employers ever read their resumes, they'll Google them."[46]

There is much to be concerned about, but my fears run deeper. How will this generation develop social skills? How will they learn to respect and trust others, the crucial building blocks of any meaningful relationship? I'm afraid that we'll raise a generation of kids who will succeed in business but fail in life because they don't know how to connect to others, to love, befriend, to care and be cared for.

Have you heard the old joke that the reason Moses brought the people to the only place in the entire Middle East that had no oil is that they refused to ask for directions? Problems of today's aging population run a whole lot deeper than not asking for directions. Older men will never ask anything of anybody. When they actually need help, they'll be terrified because they never before experienced loss of absolute control. So, they may not ask for help before it's too late because as self-made men they simply do not know how.

Everyone scrambles today to issue directives about the frightening chapter near the end of their lives. Healthcare proxies and powers of attorney are vital protections for the time when we might not be in total control of our faculties. Yet, I am convinced that the main reason that people issue end-of-life directives—no heroic measures please—is not because they know what they want when final moments approach, particularly when writing these instructions from a twenty-year distance, when death still seems an abstraction. They write these directives because they are afraid of dying alone, in pain, with nobody to help. Buber once said that he always thought he wanted to die with a book in his hand. When he got older, however, he knew that he really wanted to die with "another human hand in my own."47

Don't we all? As people grow and mature, they realize they don't want to end up alone. Yet more and more, they will lack the personal relationships they crave because they spend so little time cultivating them and thus don't have them when they need them.

That's when we really need to know we are not alone. In our congregation, we offer personal prayers for healing every Sabbath. People can call in and request prayers for loved ones and friends. The list is very long and grows all the time. Moreover, when we have completed the prayer list, we take names from the congregation. Many hands spring up. Studies abound about how much prayer assists in healing, yet I don't need conflicting studies to tell me how much people want to be prayed for. I see it every week in the number of calls and e-mails we receive and in the eyes of those ill, afraid, and in need of prayer, needing to believe as the concluding prayer of the Sabbath service says: "God is with me, I have no fear."

In these technologically driven, isolated times, we need to find God. Easier said than done for seekers who want to believe but don't know how to get there.

So, I have a four-part prescription for how to find God and thus find your true self:

*Be vulnerable. Admit that you can't do it all yourself.* At times, you even need to ask directions to know where you are truly going. Think about it this way: when you ask your kids or others significant in your life for help, you acknowledge that you don't have all the answers and neither must they. How liberating for yourself and for them. Moreover, if you seek help along the way, you won't be traumatized when you need that help later in life.

*Be awe-ful.* Look at the awesome fact that because a sperm fertilized an egg, you are alive in this world. Isn't that incredible? I'm still touched by a sermon that Rabbi Steinberg delivered over fifty years ago after a long hospitalization. Finally able to see the sunlight again, Steinberg couldn't contain himself:

After a long illness, I was permitted for the first time to step out of doors. And, as I crossed the threshold, sunlight greeted me. This is my experience—all there is to it. And yet, so long as I live, I shall never forget that moment...In that instant I looked about me to see if anyone else showed on his face the joy, almost the beatitude I felt. But no, there they walked—men and women and children in the glory of a golden flood, and so far as I could detect, there was none to give it heed. And then I remembered how often I, too, had been indifferent to sunlight, how often, preoccupied with petty and sometimes mean concerns, I had disregarded it. And I said to myself—how precious is this sunlight, but, alas, how careless of it are men. How precious—how careless. This has been a refrain sounding in me ever since.[48]

We often take these things for granted because we are afflicted with the sin of entitlement. It's all coming to us, we think, so we push aside everything precious—from people to precious sunlight—so that we can pursue ephemeral pleasures. Open your eyes to the wonder around you, and you will know one of the true secrets of the universe.

*Be grateful.* Jewish tradition requires us to say one hundred blessings every day. What if we started with one—Blessed are You, Eternal God, who has given me life. When we're young, we often think of ourselves as invincible. As our bodies age and begin to break down, we know we can take nothing for granted. A simple thank you can flip your perspective from "Why are bad things happening to me?" to "What did I do to deserve my blessings?" As an elderly grandma once put it, "I have two teeth left. Thank God they are opposite one another."[49] Grandma has a lot to teach the rest of us.

*Be purposeful.* Can I reveal another secret? You have been put on this Earth for a reason. You have a purpose. You just may not know it yet. When you invest yourself in someone or something beyond yourself, you will make a difference. When you really contribute to the repairing of our fractured world, you will discover your purpose.

Remember that wonderful little dance called the Hokey Pokey? The Hokey Pokey starts off tentatively: put your right hand in, then your left hand...right foot, then your left foot...until, finally, you put your whole self in. That feels good in the dance and everywhere else in your world. Put your whole self in, be there for others, and you will be rewarded beyond measure.

When you put your whole self in, when you find the real meaning of your life, you will find God there. God will find you there as well.

That's my best secret. Pass it on.

# CHAPTER NINE

⌒

# The Power of Prayer

PRAYER WORKS. PRAYER GETS RESULTS. In my experience, prayer can change your life and give you everything you could possibly expect from a worthwhile experience. Done right, prayer is anything but boring, passive work. On the contrary, prayer is an action plan jolting all affected parties to attention and putting them on notice that something is about to change, something important will happen. The key to successful prayer lies in understanding all that prayer can do and probably what it won't do. Having the right goals will greatly enhance the chance of success.

Let me illustrate what I mean with the help of a gumball machine. When I was a kid, I used to love to go to Arnold's Shoe Store because of a well-stocked gumball machine. Without fail, you'd put in a penny (yes, a penny), turn the handle, and out would pop a rock-hard gumball. Every time. Yet, that wasn't good enough for me. I only had eyes for that blue gumball. If the red or the green raced down the shoot, I had clearly failed.

More often than not, my hopes were dashed, but I always kept going back to that store.

The gumball machine always gave me what I needed, whether I knew it or not. Like prayer, we don't always get what we asked for or thought we needed. But if all goes well, you always want to go back to that gumball machine because you will love the result you didn't ask for or even anticipate. The result is even sweeter than the gumball because it can change the way you approach your entire life.

Let's deal up front with what prayer cannot do. Prayer does not inoculate you from all pain or misfortune. Since no one is exempt from bad things happening, since everyone dies eventually, how could prayer possibly be the magical elixir or panacea that exempts us from anything unpleasant or even tragic?

I still remember the well-dressed woman who breezily said to me, "I tried prayer once. It didn't work."

"What do you mean?" I said.

"I prayed for my grandmother to survive her stroke. She didn't."

"So was it a difficult end?"

"No, she died peacefully. In fact, she died at home at age 91."

It seems to me the prayer she should have uttered had been answered. The Talmud says that if somebody lives to the age of ninety and dies peacefully, it is as if she died kissed by God. Her grandmother received that kind of kiss. This little dialogue does illustrate, though, that if prayer is wholly results driven, and the expected result is that I and everyone else I know will be totally fine forever, no one would or should ever pray.

Secondly, prayer is no substitute for legitimate human effort. Students can pray all they want for a good grade on their science test, but it won't help at all if they spent the previous night videochatting with their friends rather than studying for the exam. Similarly, people who engage in self-destructive behavior, like insisting on driving after drinking two cocktails at a party, must take full responsibility for any consequences resulting from their irresponsible behavior. "Why did God do this to me?" may be the reflexive, tear-stained cry from their family, but, honestly, they really did it to themselves.

Close to two thousand years ago, the rabbis identified what they called a prayer said in vain, a b'racha l'vatala in Hebrew. The prayer is senseless because the words are too late to have any hope of effecting results: If a man's wife is pregnant and he says, "May God grant that my wife bear a male child," this is a vain prayer. If he is coming home from a journey and hears cries of distress from the town and says, "May God grant that this is not my house that is in trouble," this, too, is a vain prayer.

Clearly, then, there are limits to what prayer can accomplish, and the question may be asked, "If the results I can get from praying are so limited, why should I waste my time? Perhaps I should go out and do something more active?"

No one has to tell people today to be active. We are always on the move; in fact, people today are in far too big a hurry. We are runners and doers, but we don't know where we are going. We haven't identified the goals that will make our lives worth living, which will truly give us satisfaction, which will help us to look in the mirror and like who we see.

Rabbi Harold Kushner tells the story of the rabbi who once asked a prominent member of his congregation, "Whenever I see you, you are always in a hurry. Tell me, where are you running all the time?" The man answered, "I'm running after success, I'm running after fulfillment, I'm running after the reward for all my hard work."

The rabbi responded, "That's a good answer if you assume that all those blessings are somewhere ahead of you, trying to elude you and if you run fast enough you may catch up to them. But isn't it possible those blessings are behind you, that they're looking for you, and the more you run, the harder you make it for them to find you?"[50]

So prayer, first of all, forces us to stop, take a breath, and realize that as important as we think we are, as indispensable as we know we are, the world doesn't revolve around us. So much exists beyond what we can see, hear, and understand. To use an example from the world of sight, we can see so little of the entire spectrum of light that we know exists. Our optical abilities range from red on one end to violet on the other. Invisible to our eyes are the infrared wavelengths and, conversely, the ultraviolet wavelengths of the other side of the spectrum. So much of what we know is invisible to our mortal eye. This fact should generate in us a bit of humility, a sense that there is so much that we can't see and don't know. Prayer, perhaps, begins when we know we don't have all the answers and we sense a bit of awe about all that we don't know.

When the rabbis were putting together the prayer service many years ago, they knew that prayer was not going to be easy because even then, people didn't fully know who they were praying to and what they possibly could get from the experience. So, they began each prayer service by reintroducing their people to God slowly and incrementally. Intuitively, they understood that for people to pray to God successfully, the very existence of God would have to pass the plausibility test. So, they chose the theme of the first blessing prior to the Sh'ma as "God the Creator." The prayer service begins then by introducing to believers and skeptics alike the miracle of Creation:

> How manifold are your works, O God! In wisdom, You have made them all. The heavens declare Your glory. The earth reveals Your creative power. You form light and darkness, bring harmony into nature and peace to the human heart. We praise You, O God, Creator of Light.[51]

In this exultation, the rabbis are building a case for God's involvement in the world and the urge we experience to offer a prayer to that God. When you think about the world coming into existence, the prayer book asks, don't you feel a sense of wonder about it all? Don't you feel that planet Earth with all its life forces and productivity is too ordered and complex to be ushered in by some explosion of highly charged molecules, some random Big Bang? The world is so amazing that its very existence seems to defy easy scientific explanation. In fact, argue the rabbis, can you possibly imagine the spectacular planet Earth without God?

Our sages begin with this point, I believe, because if they cannot drive home the case for prayer based on awe and wonder, if they cannot sell the conviction that God is involved in our world at the inception, they will never succeed in making the sale on their next two convictions:

- God came down to reveal the law on Mount Sinai.
- God redeemed the Israelites from Egyptian bondage.

To believe that God performed these feats presupposes a faith that God somehow moved from the transcendent plane of existence to our own in order to reveal the divine plan for the world and that God truly wants to and can intervene in human history. The rabbis seemed to be initiating their followers into these possibilities step by step: if God in fact is the Creator, isn't it further possible that God revealed the Torah? If God came down to reveal sacred teachings to us, wouldn't God then have wanted to redeem us from bondage? As we have said, if you don't accept that God is the creator of the world to begin with, you are certainly not going to buy into the rest.

Prayer, then, very much rests on our ability to get beyond ourselves, to suspend our persistent skepticism, and to see wonder everywhere. At that point, it is far more likely to at least suspect that God is the reason and the source for those very miracles.

The late Jim Bishop, a well-known syndicated columnist, helps us move from appreciation of the miracle to an articulation of the belief that the only true source for miracles is God:

There is no God...

All of the wonders around you are accidental. No almighty hand made a thousand billion stars. They made themselves. No power keeps them on their steady courses. The earth magnetized itself to keep the oceans from falling off toward the sun. Infants teach themselves to cry when they are hungry or hurt. A small flower invented itself so that we could extract digitalis for sick hearts.

...Why does the earth spin at a given speed without ever slowing up, so that we have day and night? Who tilts it so that we get seasons?

...How about the sugar thermostat below the human pancreas? It maintains a level of sugar in the human blood sufficient for energy, but, without it, all of us would fall into a coma and die. No one created it. The sun stokes a fire just warm enough to sustain us on earth, but not hot enough to fry us, or cold enough to kill us.

...The human heart will beat for 70 or 80 years without faltering. How does it get sufficient rest between beats? A kidney will filter poison from the blood and leave good things alone. How does it know one from the other? Who gave the human tongue flexibility to form words, and a brain to understand them but denied it to all other animals?

...Illnesses have specific symptoms. Why this warning? Why not many illnesses with identical symptoms? Or no symptoms? Who showed a womb how to take the love of two persons and keep splitting a tiny ovum until, in time, a baby would have the proper number of fingers, eyes, ears, and hair in the right places and come into the world when it is strong enough to sustain life? Who? It's all accidental. There is no God?...[52]

If you are coming around to Bishop's view, if you are at all open to the possibility that there is a God involved in all these things, that God has in fact helped us to be on this Earth right now, then you are ready to pray.

So, what's next? Simply acknowledging your humility through the sense of wonder won't keep us praying very long. Fortunately, prayer is so much more. Prayer is an action plan for all the major parties involved. Again, prayer will never work if we think that all we need to do is petition "the man upstairs" and wait for results. The MasterCard approach to religion is doomed to failure because, at some point, inevitably, the goods will not be delivered. Prayer is certainly not about putting our order in and waiting to be served, minimal effort for minimal results. Neither is it a narcissistic exercise in feeling better about ourselves, of concentrating on our own soul in order to achieve personal satisfaction or individual salvation.

That prayer won't work.

Prayer does work, precisely because it acknowledges what the Bible contended thousands of years ago: We are put on this Earth to form an active, working relationship with God in order to do together what neither party could do on its own. Prayer not only acknowledges this relationship but energizes it, putting both sides on notice: It's time to roll up our sleeves and get to work.

When the Torah tells us "You shall be holy for God is holy," it does not tell us to adopt a passive posture of piety or go up on the mountain to meditate and commune with our personal Buddha. Holiness is an action plan. Listen to this piece of text from Leviticus, Chapter 19:

> You shall each revere his mother and his father and keep my Sabbaths: I, the Lord, am your God.
>
> Do not turn to idols or make molten gods for yourself: I, the Lord, am your God...

> When you reap the harvest of your land, you shall not reap all
> the way to the edges of your field or gather the gleanings of your
> harvest...You shall leave them both for the poor and the stranger:
> I, the Lord, am your God.
>
> You shall not steal; you shall not deal deceitfully or falsely with
> one another...You shall not defraud your neighbor. You shall not
> commit robbery. The wages of a laborer shall not remain with you
> until morning...You shall not render an unfair decision: do not
> favor the poor or show deference to the rich; judge your neigh-
> bors fairly. Do not deal basely with your fellows. Do not stand idle
> while your neighbor bleeds. I, the Lord, am your God...You shall
> love your neighbor as yourself: I am the Lord.

What the Torah is saying here is that we should perform these
actions because we were created in God's image and are trying,
however imperfectly, to imitate what God would do if God were
around. "You shall be holy, for I, the Eternal, your God, am holy"
is a statement of our potential, an invitation. Once we appreciate
our abilities, we can partner with God. We can use the rituals of
our tradition to inspire us to perform the ethical. What confidence in human beings! What an opportunity for all of us!

Prayer makes concrete this relationship, opens all of our senses
to the possibility of this relationship. Prayer must inspire us to
leave our houses of worship as different people or prayer will not
accomplish all it is able to do for us.

Prayer must lead to action or it leads to nowhere.

All right, I understand how prayer can help me repair the
world. But what about my mother stricken with cancer? How will
prayer help her?

When we offer a public prayer for healing, what we call a
Misheberach in Hebrew, we set in motion a process that engages
all concerned. First, we resolve that we will do all we can to help
the afflicted person: We will find the best doctors in order to get

the best diagnosis and treatment. Not only will we visit the sick, which, according to the rabbis, is a crucial aspect of treatment, but we will help them deal with very real practical issues, like childcare and home healthcare, and make sure that they get the very best medical care possible.

Secondly, by offering a public prayer, we alert the community to the situation and activate collective action that can bring both practical help and spiritual solace.

Finally, our collective prayer commands God's attention. God can inspire her surgeons, who in fact are healers on behalf of the Ultimate Healer. Although we never know if and how God can or will intervene directly in any one situation, God at least will know we are doing everything we can to help. We're not just sitting back on our haunches, waiting for God. Basically, we're saying if we do our part, we expect that God will do the same.

CNN reporter Dr. Sanjay Gupta tells us this story of a couple's miracle through prayer:

My husband's best friend, Hans, was supposed to be in our wedding. But three weeks before the ceremony, Hans learned he had testicular cancer. He was 38. The prognosis wasn't good. The cancer had spread to his lungs, part of his stomach, and his liver. We visited Hans a few days before we left on our honeymoon. He looked awful, and we were not optimistic that he would be alive when we returned. In a cold and dingy hospital room, we bowed our heads and prayed for our friend. The doctor who was treating Hans came into the room too, and the three of us held hands and prayed together.

By the time we got back from our honeymoon, he was sitting up in bed. Six weeks later, he would walk out of that hospital, minus part of his lung, and he would live way beyond the number of years the doctors had given him. I believe it was a miracle. Now, I have another friend who is a Harvard-educated scientist who will tell you that no miracle took place. He's an atheist and believes that everything that happens can be explained scientifically. He would say that God didn't save Hans, but rather, the doctors did. In many ways, I can't argue. Hans was treated with a cutting-edge vaccine designed to fight testicular cancer, much like Lance Armstrong's treatment. But there was something in that room the night we prayed that makes me believe it was more than just a vaccine that kept Hans alive. I believe prayer, hope, and faith had an awful lot to do with his healing.

Plenty of studies have been done on the effects of prayer. A good many have found that those with faith tend to be healthier. But other studies have found no such effect. Researchers at Duke University, in one of the largest studies ever conducted on prayer and healing, found no difference in the recovery of heart patients who had prayer, compared with those who didn't. And regardless of religion—Buddhist, Muslim, Jewish, or Christian— their outcome was about the same.

Around this time of Easter, I often think of our friend Hans. I will always remember him as a man who taught me an awful lot about prayer and healing. I feel when fighting an illness, you have to believe something or someone will help you through it. For Hans, I think it was his strong will to live and his beliefs. For my friend from Harvard, who has fought clinical depression most of his life, it's the medicine he takes every day. But I will never forget that day in the hospital, when three people joined to ask for help from a higher power. I believe prayer works.

What do you think?...Do you think prayer helps heal the sick? [53]

Of course, there have been a number of studies concerning prayer's effects on healing. Some state definitively that prayer produces results; others state the opposite conclusion. I'm not impressed with such studies because I don't know how realistic those expectations are in the first place. If the studies are about whether prayer by itself will take care of the illness, the results will be disappointing. If the study asks whether prayer, which activates all these interdependent forces, can help the stricken, I know the answer is a resounding yes. I know this because of how many people call to be put on our prayer list at my own congregation. The number grows exponentially every week. Whenever I visit people in the hospital or call them on the phone hours before surgery asking if they would like me to pray with them, the answer is always yes. People tell me constantly that my prayers sustained them through the surgery and then the arduous weeks of recovery.

I would note, too: Prayer need not be a calming experience. Since this is an active relationship between the human and divine realms, our prayer can be challenging, demanding, subversive even. The Bible makes clear that God wanted to engage us this way. In the very beginning of the Torah, when God wanted to destroy the cities of Sodom and Gomorrah, God told Abraham about the plans. Why did God do this? If God wanted to destroy cities, God certainly didn't need the approval of Abraham. Clearly, God sought a strong reaction from Abraham, wanted Abraham to challenge the decision on grounds of justice. Abraham did not disappoint.

What if there are innocent people in the town, he thundered. What if there are fifty, forty-five, forty, all the way down to ten righteous people. Shall the judge of all the earth not do justice?

The Torah is clearly modeling the type of relationship it believes God wants from us: a dynamic and often difficult inter-playing, with each side challenging the other, pushing the other, demanding the maximum from each other. For this to work, we have to be present. Prayer invites us into that fully engaged relationship, to feel that all parties involved can do more to repair a broken body or a fractured world.

Prayer expects us to feel gratitude but also to feel indignation about inequality, sickness, malnutrition, people dying of preventable diseases. Prayer underscores the very real conviction that God and we need each other. God, too, is needy. One of the ways we know this is, according to the Talmud, God also prays:

> May it be My will that My mercy suppresses My anger, and that it may prevail over My attributes of justice and judgment, and that I might deal with My children according to the attributes of compassion, and that I may not act towards them according to the strict course of justice. (Babylonian Talmud, Berachot 7a)

In my judgment, God's mercy will be triggered by our own. Prayer, then, is a call to action, a heartfelt intention to bring mercy to God's children, hoping that God's mercy will follow in response.

Prayer works because it is an action plan making all parties better than they would have been otherwise. Prayer works because it produces results. We are charged to live up to our potential. We are inspired to be all we can be, fully human, people created in the image of God.

The celebrated actor Charles Laughton tells the story about being invited to participate in the Sunday morning service of a little English country church where he happened to be vacationing. Since he was blessed with a magnificent voice, Laughton chose to deliver the 23rd Psalm in booming tones and recited it so movingly that the entire congregation burst into applause.

He was followed by an elderly, feeble friar, who stepped up to the pulpit and in a shaking voice recited the same Psalm. When he concluded, there wasn't a dry eye in the sanctuary. All had been profoundly moved.

After the service, Laughton's manager asked him to explain why they reacted so much more deeply to the old man, and Laughton replied, "I'll tell you the difference. While I know the words of the 23rd Psalm very well, that old man over there, he knows the shepherd."

So can we. Through prayer. Prayer works. Prayer works if we do more than mouth the words. Prayer is a call to action. Prayer puts us all on full alert, a signal from us to God that we're coming— we're coming with full resources of head, heart, and soul and expect God to do the same. We're coming as engaged partners in the often Herculean joint effort to make this bloodstained, unjust globe more peaceful and fair than we ever dared hope it could be.

That's truly something to pray for; in fact, something to live for.

# CHAPTER TEN

*~~~~~*

# Why God Should Not Choose the Next President

EXCITEMENT BUILDS TO A FEVER pitch in the crowded auditorium. The presidential candidate is beaming as he is about to receive an endorsement that will give his campaign unprecedented momentum. While he is addressing the crowd, however, no one is paying him the slightest attention. Their eyes are riveted on the very spot where none other than Jesus Christ, the superstar, would enter the room to thunderous applause. Americans of all political and religious persuasion were there to witness Christ's return to Earth.

In the back of the auditorium sat populations of poor people—whites, blacks, Latinos—some with the callused hands of folks who work for a living and the tired eyes of those who have been ground down by life. They were there to be lifted up by the Jesus of hope and liberation, the Christ who understood their misery like no one else because he had truly been there. In front of them, black Baptists swayed to the music. Christ was coming, and they were there in full-throated witness to God's glory. The Religious Right was out in force and pleased as punch with what was about to happen. They had possessed the Truth for a long time, and now Christ would affirm that sacred fact for the entire world. Having seen God with their own eyes and heard God with their own ears, people would want God to suffuse every aspect of life. Now returning God to the public arena would be accomplished by affirmation. Prayer would now begin every school day. Evolution would permanently be banned as godless blasphemy. Finally, the goal of making the United States a Christian nation with "pro-life" values would be achieved with a single appearance of the Lord Jesus.

At the far right sat hardcore fundamentalists who were waiting for Christ their warrior to lead them in the ultimate End of Days battle against the Antichrist. Christ's appearance was the signal: Armageddon is at hand, Rapture is around the corner. Messianic fervor could scarcely be contained.

Scattered around the audience sat an incognito, ashen-faced group of non-Christians—Jews, Muslims, secularists, atheists, and, of course, representatives of the ACLU, who, in shock, wondered who had hijacked their constitution. Hadn't the Founding Fathers fully understood the dangers of the state becoming subservient to the church? Hadn't the alliance between church and state in England been the source of so much prejudice and discord that the wall of separation had to be put in place here to protect the state? As Alan Dershowitz effectively argues in his book called *Blasphemy*, the United States was not ever to be a Christian country. The Declaration of Independence in fact was an "anticlerical document that elevated nature, science, and human reason over 'monkish ignorance and superstition.'"[54] God was never invoked in the Constitution at all, and the only time religion is mentioned is to ensure that there would be no religious test to qualify for public office.

If you are convinced you do not believe in God, or you are questioning your belief, or you are struggling to find your way back, you probably welcome the wall of separation. Clearly, such a separation still permits people to believe as they wish and still bring religious values to bear on their own way of life and political views. At the same time, the wall of separation, rigidly enforced, was designed to make sure that the views of the majority would never trample upon those of the minority. Never again would those who don't believe in God or Christ as the son of God have to feel that they are less American because of those views.

So, pray tell, how did this auditorium scenario come to pass? Truth be told, virtually all candidates for America's highest office today would welcome God at their side. Both Republicans and Democrats are expected not only to hold religious beliefs but to discuss them publicly. How their religion influences their lives and how they would govern must be incorporated into the standard stump speech. This is understandable in a country in which 80 percent of respondents say they believe in God. Requiring candidates to come clean about their faith could be found on page one of almost any campaign director's playbook.

Despite the wishes of the Founding Fathers, religious faith has always been a driving force in American political life. North American colonies were a religious refuge for people all across Europe, and the ruling powers were more than willing to get rid of their dissidents. No surprise, then, to find a high ratio of churchgoers and many more denominations here than Europe ever had encompassed.[55] As Kevin Phillips documents, both in the American Revolution and the Civil War, religion was often a decisive factor in how people chose sides in the conflict. Colonial parishioners who were descendants of the Church of England divided loyalty along high-church, low-church lines. High-church Anglicans, especially in New England, New York, and New Jersey, supported the Crown. Low-church Anglicans, like the planters of Virginia and the Carolinas, supported the Revolution. By 1861, the United States had become the world's most Christian nation.[56] By any measure, it still is.

Why shouldn't Christ appear where he is so popular? All those who believe that they are now the chosen people in this blessed land were about to be validated. After all, Christ was coming to them. Anticipation was approaching fever pitch. What would he say? What political system does he advocate? What are his political preferences? Who would he endorse? Who, after all, is the real Jesus?

Scholars and clerics have asked that very question for over two thousand years. Since the New Testament and Jesus's pronouncements are so much based on his Jewish background and upon the Hebrew Bible, it is important to first ask what political views the so-called Old Testament would dictate to its devotees. What, for example, would Moses advocate?

While Moses followed his father-in-law Jethro's advice and appointed representatives from all the tribes to be leaders of groups of one thousand, one hundred, fifty, and ten, capable, honest men who fear God and refuse to take bribes (Exodus 18:1), Jethro was not an advocate of democracy as a political ideal. His suggestion was a practical measure because Moses could not personally handle all the disputes that were likely to arise.

In any case, representative government could be viewed as a temporary measure. Moses's real focus is less upon what happens to the people in the desert than what happens to them when they enter the Promised Land without him. The Bible's assumption is that the people will want to imitate the people around them:

> When you take over the land and settle there, you may think, "we
> should select a king to rule over us like the other nations around
> us." If this happens, be sure to select as king the man whom the
> Lord chooses...The king must not accumulate large amounts of
> wealth and silver and gold for himself. When he sits on the
> throne he must copy for himself this body of instruction, the
> Torah, on a scroll in the presence of the levitical priests. He must
> always keep that copy with him and read it daily as long as he
> lives. That way he will learn to fear the Lord, thy God, by obeying
> all the terms of these instructions and decrees. (Deuteronomy 17)

Neither the monarch nor the people will possess ultimate
power. God is the real authority, and their job is to obey His
covenant. Moses's biggest fear, articulated as virtual certainty,
concerns the time when the people enter the land and when
their curiosity may lead them to follow the practices of neigh-
boring peoples. Worse, they may want to assimilate by worship-
ping their gods, thereby abrogating the covenant. Not only
would such worship represent rejection of the God who brought
them out of Egypt, such behavior would reflect incredible arrogance born of material success. It would also signify their
embrace of the abhorrent, immoral practices that are a direct
outgrowth of such idolatrous worship:

> When you enter the land which the Lord, your God is giving
> you, be very careful not to imitate the despicable customs of the
> nations living there. For example, never sacrifice your son or
> daughter as a burnt offering. (Deuteronomy 18:9–10)

> They burn them as a sacrifice to the gods. (Deuteronomy 13:31)

The survival and well-being of not only the people and the
covenant but perhaps of God Himself are at stake, so ample

rewards and devastating punishments are laid out as direct consequences for covenantal compliance and rejection. Justice is the
supreme value to be exercised in matters big and small. Poverty is
to be eliminated. Every third year, a second tithe is to be offered
so that the levites, foreigners, orphans, and widows will have
enough to eat in their towns. (Deuteronomy 26:12)

Clearly, our ancestors seem entirely comfortable in a free enter-
prise system. The text assumes that some people will be more
successful than others: "When you have become prosperous and
have built fine houses to live in, when your flocks and herds have
become larger and silver and gold have multiplied, don't say 'I've
achieved this wealth by the might of my own hand.'"

Gratitude to God will impel the wealthy to eliminate poverty in
their midst. Voluntary compliance seems to be the modus
operandi rather than legislative fiat: "If there are poor Israelites in
your towns...don't be hard-hearted or tight-fisted toward them.
Instead, be generous and lend them whatever they need."
(Deuteronomy 15)

Moses's primary focus concerns building a nation that would be
an embodiment of the covenant. Moses doesn't yet have the
luxury of a universalistic view. To embrace the universal for him
at this early stage of Israelite life is to risk losing the particular
while decimating the Bible's vision that the people of Israel and
its covenant would serve as a moral beacon surrounded by
immoral, bloodthirsty peoples and their gods. The promise of
Sinai is that the people would become a "kingdom of priests and
a holy nation." Sadly, the people's practices left them far short of
the goal. Since Moses would not enter the Promised Land, he
could only hope that the people would have the discipline to
resist internal and external temptations to stray from their
purpose and perhaps disappear due to their own moral turpitude.
Yet, Moses reaches the sobering realization that before they could
be a holy nation, they first had to be a nation.

If Moses's political views were based on fears of the unknown future, Jesus's worldview had to be based on the concrete reality of an oppressive present. In the year 63 B.C.E., when General Pompey marched into Israel, the Romans proceeded to economically starve, plunder, rape, and slaughter thousands of inhabitants. The historian Josephus recounts that around the time Jesus was born, the Roman military crucified some two thousand people in the Galilean city of Sepphoris as punishment for rebelling against Roman rule.[57] If their own brutality was not enough, they installed a descendant of the Maccabean clan, Herod, as "King of the Jews," who proceeded to do Rome's bidding in completing the subjugation of the people, particularly in Galilee, Jesus's birthplace, and in Jerusalem.

Desperate times evoke a full range of responses both from mainstream political entities and from more fringe elements, who, in these trying circumstances, have a better chance of gaining the attention of the besieged population. Among the establishment parties lived the Sadducees. They were social and political conservatives who tried to work with Rome and uphold the status quo. The Sadducees benefited from the taxation that flowed into the priestly coffers. Their political opponents, the Pharisees, had looser ties to the establishment and felt freer to operate outside the strictures of Torah law. From the Sadducean view, God's word was found in Scriptures and nowhere else. The Pharisees established the view that side by side with the written law, an oral tradition was established as integral to the very idea of Torah.

Thus, the Pharisees opened the minds of the people to integrate other ideas prevalent in the Greco-Roman world, like the immortality of the soul and the world to come. Clearly, some Pharisees reacted to Roman rule by turning inward and emphasizing personal piety. Others became aligned with the Zealots, whose response to Rome was a militant one. Determined to resist to the death, they forced Rome to bring to Jerusalem many more brigades of troops than they ever dreamed necessary. Other groups, like the Essenes, took the exact opposite tact and withdrew into the desert to live a more serene, spiritual life.

The desperate need for a messiah emerges among the Israelites at times when oppressive persecution persists and people lose faith both in God and their political leaders. In such circumstances, they seek a redeemer who can instantly offer relief from ever-present anguish.

Was Jesus of Nazareth the messiah? Was he an establishment figure who aligned himself with a segment of society? Or did he advocate withdrawal from the political and social realities of his time in order to find a new way that would ease the suffering of the poor and the downtrodden?

Identifying the historic Jesus—who he was and what he stood for—may be history's most difficult challenge. Beyond dispute is the fact that no one who wrote about or quoted Jesus ever met him. The authors of the four Gospels were not eyewitnesses to history and wrote anywhere from thirty to eighty years' distance from the life and times of Jesus of Nazareth. Paul, who is more responsible than anyone for turning his story into a new faith, knew nothing of Jesus in the flesh. Alas, these sources are basically all we have, and we must rely on the knowledge that those who lived close to the history they chronicled may be reporting these events more accurately than any other source we possess.

Indeed, we will learn about Jesus from the New Testament or we will know nothing at all. Neither the Hebrew Bible nor the New Testament is objective history, but rather, these works would serve to entice people into their own covenantal understanding. Nevertheless, we need to use these precious sources because, for example, if we have some understanding of Jesus's interaction with his own world, we might have better insights into what he would advocate in ours.

Without question, Jesus did not attract the loving attention in first-century Palestine that he would get today. Indeed, in this volatile, terror-filled region, any new leader with significant backing would be seen as threatening to the existing authority. Make no mistake about it: Jesus was a charismatic personality who could attract a crowd. Stories about his ability to heal abounded and produced both growing fascination and concern in many spiritual and political circles.

King Herod, who had been given the title King of the Jews by Rome, must have been driven mad by the wise men from the East who arrived in Jerusalem to herald Jesus's coming, "Who is He, who has been born King of the Jews? For we have seen His star in the East and have come to worship Him." (Matthew 2:2) From the Roman emperor to the Jewish "King," everyone could legitimately feel threatened by the arrival of this "star from the East."

Surely every political group vacillated between wanting to co-opt Jesus and undermine him. Their concern seemed to be justified, for Jesus brought to this brewing stew an entirely different worldview that would make it virtually impossible for him to align with any current political movement. His simple agenda was stated clearly as he stood before the Roman procurator in Jerusalem, Pontius Pilate, and said, "My Kingdom is not of this world."

His solution was not to make social change within existing reality, nor was it a withdrawal into the desert. Jesus was imploring every member of the Jewish people to commit not only to the ethical standards of the Torah but to moral behaviors that would far exceed them. Everyone who faithfully committed to that agenda would contribute to a momentum that would ultimately create what he called "the Kingdom of Heaven," which is not in some messianic era yet to come nor an actual location in the heavens. For Jesus, the Kingdom of Heaven was more of a mind-set, which can happen right here where people live. If individuals do gain entrance into the kingdom, then what happens in the harsh, brutal world where people actually live is much less relevant because they have already transcended the relatively petty concerns of mammon.

Thus, we can understand Jesus's pivotal Sermon on the Mount using this very context:

> For I say to you, that unless your righteousness exceed the righteousness of the scribes and Pharisees, you'll by no means enter the Kingdom of Heaven...
>
> You have heard it said, "You shall not commit adultery." But I say to you that whoever even looks at a woman, to lust after her, has already committed adultery with her in his heart...
>
> You have heard it said that, "An eye for an eye and a tooth for a tooth." But I tell you to resist an evil pass. Whoever strikes you on the right cheek, turn the other to him also. If anyone wants to take away your tunic, let him have your coat also...
>
> You have heard it said, "You shall love your neighbor and hate your enemy." But I say to you, love your enemies—do good to those who hate you. (Matthew 5:20–44)

Clearly, this is a clarion call for ethical behavior above and beyond any previous call to duty. Not only will it move its adherents into the Kingdom of Heaven but will inspire a desire in others to want to gain entrance as well.

Jesus's parables were designed to build this very momentum. "The Kingdom of Heaven is like a mustard seed which a man sows in his field. This is the least of seeds, but when it grows, it is greater than the herbs and becomes a tree, so that the birds come and nestle in its branches." (Matthew 13:31–32)

Jesus clearly believed that the Kingdom of Heaven was a vital spiritual refuge from the harsh realities on the ground. In my judgment, the reason why Jesus never specifically denied to any ruling power that he was the King of the Jews or the messiah is not that he actually believed it to be the case, but he did not want to dilute his influence among the population he was hoping to win over. His was a campaign to win souls for the Kingdom of Heaven, his life's mission, and he needed them to reorient their worldview to seek spiritual rather than political goals.

Now we can fully understand why Jesus never counseled militant actions aimed at the ruling powers: "Render unto Caesar the things that are Caesar's and to God the things that are God's," he taught. (Matthew 22:21) For Jesus, those who enter the Kingdom of Heaven are immune to Caesar's power and are able to transcend all the suffering they have experienced.

Without a doubt, Jesus saw that suffering with his own eyes, but he seemed to have no interest in the political work that might bring about needed social change. "Give us this day our daily bread and forgive us our debts" (Matthew 6:11–12) was not a political clarion call for him but a benefit of the Kingdom of Heaven. What they lack in this kingdom is more than made up for in the next.

Assuming that the authors of the Gospels accurately captured Christ's agenda, modern-day followers of Christ, such as those who are now awaiting his arrival in the auditorium, may understandably grow more restless. Jesus Christ's goals were simply not in concert with their goals. Those who had been anticipating Christ the warrior to lead them in the battle of Armageddon fretted that Jesus of Nazareth would want the focus not on the End of Days but on gaining entrance to the Kingdom of Heaven through renewed spiritual and ethical growth this very day. That's not the Christ they wanted to see.

Those who were hoping that Christ would trigger a messianic movement to end poverty would be disappointed to know that Jesus would not be participating in the political process at all but would only promise fulfillment of these worthy goals in another realm. Why enter the grimy political marketplace when everything will be in order once we leave behind this place in our minds and hearts?

Social conservatives were now in a panic. Who is this guy anyway? This is not the Jesus Christ they've always known. He doesn't even seem to have the same unfettered passion for the things he's supposed to care about.

Prayer in the public schools? Not interested.

Abortion as murder? Never thought about it.

Indeed, anti-abortion crusaders were particularly crestfallen. They needed Jesus's personal endorsement because despite pious protestations to the contrary, they never had Scripture on their side. Despite their best efforts to twist the contextual meanings of both Old and New Testament writings, there are no verses whatsoever that outlaw abortion or even come close.

Ironically, in the one episode in the entire Bible in which an abortion takes place, the results do not endorse the pro-lifer's stance: "If men fight and hurt a woman who is pregnant, so that her fruit depart from her but no other damage ensues, he shall be punished according to what the woman's husband can negotiate and shall pay as the judges determine." (Exodus 21)

If the fetus were a human being, if life begins at conception, the penalty would have been death based on the "eye for eye" standard of justice. Precisely because the fetus is not yet a full human being, a crisis has happened here, a tragedy has occurred, but murder is not charged.

Pro-lifers, of course, don't want to hear this. They want to know only the Christ they have projected, not the Christ who will soon appear before them. So rather than wait for the curtain to rise, social conservatives are starting to leave the hall, lest they hear the Truth, which will undermine the only truth they have ever known.

All these folks will be relieved to know that Jesus Christ never did take the stage. Sadly, they would rather live with the illusion that what they bring to the Bible and religion is the correct interpretation. Don't bother me with the facts, don't bother me with context about the real Moses or Christ or what they would advocate for our times. We have the truth! Who cares what he would have said?

Once again, do not blame God for what some people do in the name of God. All the delegates in the hall would benefit from the key point made by Moses and Jesus: God calls us to a standard of conduct, a morality that we will never attain without God. Both spiritual leaders point to the need to treat each other with extraordinary compassion, which often forces us to act not as everyone else does but to separate ourselves from the immorality around us to attain a level of ethical living that can actually change the world.

Without God, there is no ultimate moral standard. Without God, we are free to do what we want, hoping not to get caught, able to rationalize that, after all, everyone else is doing it, so what the hell?

If Jesus had entered the hall that day, he very well might have said what he was quoted as saying to the leaders of his own day: "You have a way of rejecting the commandments of God so that you may keep your own tradition." (Mark 7:9)

So many people in our midst care more about what they want God to say to them than what God is actually saying. But Moses and Jesus both maintained a belief in their people and felt that they could ultimately rise above the mean standards of the world and actually live up to their potential.

They believed in us because, as the Bible maintains, God made a remarkable decision to fashion us in the image of God, capable of acting as God would act if He walked among us.

If we ever come close to that behavior, then, and only then, will we humans create our own brand of the "Kingdom of Heaven" right here, right now, on planet Earth.

# CHAPTER ELEVEN

⟜⟝

# Making Miracles Matter

*IDDLER ON THE ROOF'S* **TEVYE** was a poor dairyman from a poor village. Somehow, he saw miracles "large and small" everywhere. People today, often much more materially blessed than Tevye, regularly complain that they have never even seen a miracle. What gives? Have miracles somehow disappeared, did God appear on the Earth in a miraculous star turn at the time of Moses and Jesus, then, having established a good reputation, stopped performing them for the likes of you and me?

Not according to the poet Walt Whitman. In his poem *Miracles*, he writes:

Why, who makes much of a miracle?
As to me, I know of nothing else but miracles,
Whether I walk the streets of Manhattan,
Or dart my sight over the roofs of houses toward the sky,

Or wade with naked feet along the beach just in the edge
    of the water,
Or stand under trees in the woods,
Or talk by day with any one I love, or sleep in the bed at
    night with any one I love,
Or sit at table at dinner with the rest...
Or animals feeding in the fields,
Or birds, or the wonderfulness of insects in the air,
Or the wonderfulness of the sundown, or of stars shining
    so quiet and bright,
Or the exquisite delicate thin curve of the new moon in
    spring;...
These with the rest, one and all, are to me miracles

Einstein once said, "There are only two ways to live life. One is as though nothing is a miracle. The other is as though everything is."

So, are miracles everywhere or nowhere?

In the *Book of Miracles,* author Kenneth Woodward, the former religion editor at *Newsweek,* defines a miracle as: "An unusual or extraordinary event that is in principle perceivable by others, that finds no reasonable explanation in ordinary human abilities or in other known forces that operate in the world of time and space, and that is the result of a special act of God."[58]

In the biblical period, supernatural miracles seemed almost a prerequisite to human action. Moses was aroused to duty through a burning bush in which God "speaks" in order to convince Moses that he must return to Egypt as a liberator. At the behest of God, Moses will perform miraculous feats of magic before mortal enemies like Pharaoh and natural obstacles like the Sea of Reeds. Many years later, according to the New Testament, Jesus is directly involved in at least thirty-five miraculous occurrences.

So what happened? Why was the world so full of God's miraculous deeds back then, but today there is, in the minds of many people, no evidence of miracles in our midst?

In my judgment, God has always acted in similar fashion throughout history. I don't believe that God made a splash back in biblical times and then disappeared from the world stage. In fact, I believe that miracles were manifest regularly in biblical times and are manifest regularly in modern times as well. God's presence in the world hasn't changed one bit. Seeing miracles may very well depend on us. There is no chance of finding miracles if our senses aren't alert, aware of the absolute awesomeness around us. The beauty is that you don't have to be in front of a burning bush or walking through divided waters or watching the curing of lepers to be the recipient of a miracle.

Miracles may arrive even when you're still in your bathrobe:

Olivia had been battling addiction to alcohol and barbiturates for as long as she could remember. Divorced for many years, Olivia looked forward to the birth of her first grandchild. So, she busied herself with knitting a hat, buying gifts, and preparing for the call that would put her on a plane and into orbit as the happiest grandmother on Earth.

The call never came. Not wanting to be an intrusive mother, she held off calling her daughter, all the while wondering if she would be dilating and preparing to deliver.

One day, she could control herself no longer and placed the call. Her daughter Sharon answered with a quick hello and awkward silence.

"Sharon, is everything all right?"

"Everything is fine, Mom. Tom and I had a baby girl last week. Seven pounds, two ounces. She's really beautiful!"

"Last week, Sharon? Why didn't you call me? I've been ready to fly out for weeks. Why didn't you call me?"

Silence again. "Well, Mom, Tom and I decided we really didn't want you here. Frankly, you've been an incredible load for us to handle. We didn't want to impose that on us or the baby."

Olivia hung up stunned. Sure, there had been some tension between her and her daughter, particularly after her marriage with Tom, whom Olivia regarded with disdain and suspicion. Nothing, however, prepared her for such total rejection.

Too ashamed to face the well-meaning questions of her friends, Olivia retreated into her apartment. Drugs and drink became a steady diet and her only companions. Calls to Sharon landed on the answering machine; e-mails were not returned. Olivia became more and more distraught. One morning, with shades still drawn, she stumbled into the bathroom, unscrewed a bottle of pills, and was about to swallow its full contents.

At that very moment, she heard a loud knock at the front door. Hurriedly, she threw on her robe, splashed water on her face, and hustled to open the door.

There stood her college roommate, Terri, whom she had not seen in at least ten years.

"Didn't you get the message that I was coming to the city for a meeting and that I wanted to see you after all these years?"

Olivia and Terri just stared at each other for a long time. Neither could quite comprehend that, unwittingly, Terri had saved Olivia's life that morning. Arriving at precisely the right moment after not seeing her roommate for ten years, Terri was the human agent for a true miracle. Was that miracle heaven sent, God's working through human beings to effect the needed result? Was Terri's arrival a "natural" occurrence, a coincidence, rather than a supernatural intervention?

If miracles do happen, who is empowered to perform them, and what is the source of their power to be miracle-makers? To make that judgment, let's go back to our major source of miracles—our bibles—to get this perspective on the where, why, how, and who of miracle production.

The quintessential miracle-maker is clearly Jesus of Nazareth. By all accounts, he needed this ability because according to the Gospels, Jesus's arrival on the scene in the Holy Land was initially greeted not by acclaim but cynicism. When Jesus came to Capernaum in Galilee, the crowds eagerly brought him a paralyzed man for healing. When Jesus said to the afflicted fellow, "Son, your sins are forgiven you," some among the crowd scoffed. They came to see healing, but Jesus offered mere repentance! Others charged Jesus with blasphemy, saying that only God can forgive sins, so what gives you the right to declare that this man's sins are forgiven?

Jesus persisted: "I saved you, so arise, get out of the bed and go your way to your house." Immediately, the man arose and walked out to the clear surprise of the entire crowd. They were totally amazed and instantly glorified God, saying, "We never saw anything like this." (Mark 2:11)

Notice that in this early appearance in Galilee, Jesus performed miracles with no reference to God's power. In his own mind, he was seemingly no mere extension of God's transcendent power. It is as if Jesus had to establish his own bona fides so that he would eventually gain credibility to speak in the name of God. Here, the people immediately glorify God in the face of the miracle. Jesus, as yet, does not.

While later teaching and spreading prophecy in Nazareth, Jesus performs an incredible feat of feeding four thousand hungry people with only seven loaves of bread. Thus, his reputation grew.

The Pharisees, one of the leading political parties among the Jews, began to challenge his power and authenticity. Testing this new prophet, they demanded a sign from him. Pointedly, Jesus did not accommodate their request but challenged them in turn, "Why does this generation seek a sign? Assuredly, I say to you, no sign shall be given to this generation."

This is a stunning reply. The Pharisees sought assurance that Jesus was acting as an actual extension of God's reach, but Jesus would provide no such assurance. As the purported Son of God, Jesus could have made clear that everything he did was divinely engineered. His response, to the contrary, seemed to make clear that the power to perform miracles can be found in the realm of human authority.

This point was reinforced when John, one of Jesus's disciples, approached him, saying, "Teacher, we saw someone who was not following us casting out demons in your name, and we forbad him because he does not follow us."

But Jesus said, "Do not forbid him, for one who works a miracle in my name afterward cannot speak evil of me. For he who is not against us is on our side." (Mark 9:38–41)

The author of this Gospel certainly never insists that these are divine actions. This is understandable because the writer, living at least forty years after the event, was neither an eyewitness to history nor privy to the theological view that Christ, as part of a trinity, was not only sent by God but was actually an integral part of God.

Even more curious is the fact that Jesus of Nazareth does not feel the need to invoke God as the author and authority of the miracle. Again, the text seems more concerned with establishing Jesus's wide-ranging abilities to perform acts that bedazzle the senses and defy explanation.

Perhaps the New Testament wants to celebrate miracles as possible human manifestations of the Bible's teaching that we were created in the divine image. More profoundly, Scripture may be speaking to us about our role in doing God's work here on Earth. This brings to mind a delightful story that the famed Reform Jewish teacher and mystic Lawrence Kushner once taught:

> The richest man in the village once dozed off during services. [As a rabbi, I am of course shocked about this, but it is not my story.]

As he was starting to wake up, he vaguely heard the Torah discussion describing the commandment to offer challah as a sacrifice to the Temple. Now fully awake, he is convinced that God was speaking directly to him, commanding him to bring challahs to the synagogue. So, right before Shabbat he does precisely that and, wanting to leave them as close to God as possible, he places them in the Holy Ark.

Meanwhile, the poorest man in the village who made a little money cleaning up the synagogue every Friday walks in and begins to pray, "Dear God, I am so poor. I have nothing to feed my family. I have never asked you for anything, but now I need your help." With a sigh he opens the ark to continue his cleaning when, lo and behold, he finds there twelve loaves of bread. He cannot believe the miracle that is occurring before his eyes. This little drama continues for a period of weeks until the rabbi discovers what is going on and brings the two men together. Both understood what happened but both feared that God no longer would be a power in their lives as they had assumed.

Shaking his head, the rabbi asks them to look at their hands. "Your hands," he said to the rich man, "are the hands of God giving food to the needy. Your hands," said the rabbi to the poor man, "are also the hands of God receiving that which was intended for you." [59]

This story teaches me that God may very often be the author of miracles, but they will not take place if we are not there carrying them out, if our senses are not open to the possibility of receiving the very same miracle.

When God sends biblical Moses back to free the Hebrew slaves from bondage, it was Moses who had the tricks up his sleeve. Moses was the one who could turn his staff into a snake or produce leprosy from his chest when none had previously existed. It is not so shocking that the Egyptian magicians could duplicate these feats, so God had to ratchet up the manifestation of divine power. Soon the horrific plagues were mandated and produced by God but again had to be proffered by human deliverymen.

Interestingly enough, both Moses and Jesus increasingly introduced God's authority as their own personal reputations grew. For almost four hundred years, God alone, seemingly, could not convince the slaves in Egypt to want their freedom enough to do something about it. God needed Moses and his brother Aaron to convince the people of God's power to effect salvation. The miracle was never the goal; the miracle inspired people to pay attention to the task expected of them at Sinai: ratifying the covenant made between a people and a God through the gift of Torah.

For Jesus, too, miracles were designed to get people to pay attention to his message, a prophetic plea for them to want to enter the Kingdom of God, Jesus's vision of heaven on Earth.

Jesus clearly knew that his target audience, the Jews, might appreciate the miracle as a source of authority. After all, didn't Moses employ miracles to establish his proper role as a leader of the people? This prophet wanted them to embrace personal ethical mandates based on Torah, which in many cases superseded Torah's standards in order to enter the selective Kingdom of God. Far better would it have been for the Jews to accept the Kingdom on personal faith, but Jesus knew they were coming from a skeptical place and that his very persona would have to convince them to shift their spiritual orientation. If miracles at first produced skepticism, by the sheer number and magnitude, Jesus began to establish enough credibility to get people to pay attention. Then, and only then, perhaps, would they open their minds to a new and somewhat different covenantal understanding.

So miracles are important, crucial in fact, for advancing God's plan on Earth, both from the Christian and Jewish points of view. Clearly, human beings are essential players in producing the miracle that will advance the larger divine goals here on Earth.

Judaism, in fact, has a holiday based on a miracle, made possible by the work of the few who defied their oppressors. Every Jewish kindergarten student knows the story of the military victory of Judah the Maccabee, his brothers, and followers over the Syrian Greeks, who had defiled the Temple with idolatrous religious figures and of the miraculous discovery of the oil that burned for eight days and nights. If it's hard enough to understand how a whole holiday could sprout from a tiny jar of oil, your skepticism will deepen when you discover that the Books of Maccabees, the primary sources for this narrative, know nothing of this vial of oil or even of the Chanukah miracle. That tale is told in the Babylonian Talmud edited over six hundred years after these historical events:

> What is Chanukah about? Our rabbis taught, "When the Greeks entered the Temple, they defiled all the oils therein. After the Hasmonean Dynasty prevailed and defeated them, they searched and found only one cruse of oil which still had on it the seal of the High Priest (therefore untouched and pure). This little bottle contained enough oil for only one day's illumination. Then a miracle occurred when the lamp remained lit for eight days. Ultimately, these eight days are commemorated in the festival of Chanukah with recitation of prayers of praise (Hallel) and thanksgiving. (Babylonian Talmud, Shabbat 21b)

Chanukah, then, was based on a miracle that was not reported contemporaneous with the Maccabean victory but added to the historic record many hundreds of years later. Why does the Talmud do this? My guess is that the rabbis feared that the people had become all too comfortable with the belief that their fates rest on their military might and political savvy.

Don't rely on secular yardsticks, utterly rational explanations, the rabbis countered. They will disappoint you. In fact, they argued, God fashioned a great miracle and can do so again.

Make no mistake about it, however: Even the rabbis did not believe that God could fashion this miracle alone. Part and parcel of this miracle was the fact that an obscure priest from a small town stood up to the government that wanted to undermine religious and political freedom. Judah the Maccabee's father had no way of knowing that members of the highly assimilated Jewish elite would fight an undermanned and underarmed guerrilla war against the Syrian Greeks. Their resolve was part of the miracle. Pointedly, the Pietists who recaptured the Temple waited at least two months for divine restoration of the Temple rite. When no such divine intervention came, the Maccabees and their followers understood the interconnection between human effort and divine intervention. The miracle of oil would have never occurred without the Maccabees proceeding to cleanse the Temple and restore God's central place in the religious life of the people. The oil burned for eight days only because committed human beings first kindled the oil. Thus, a great miracle happened there because God's children helped make it so.

Undoubtedly, the most dramatic miracle in all biblical history is the parting of the Sea of Reeds. Following the climactic rescue of the Israelites in Egypt, Moses led the people northeast toward the Promised Land of Canaan. Momentarily stunned by the plagues, which God employed to punish Egypt, the Pharaoh now changed his mind and sent a large army riding horse-drawn chariots to force the Jews to return to his kingdom. With Pharaoh's soldiers pursuing them, the fleeing Israelites finally arrived at the menacing Sea of Reeds. Overcome with panic, they found themselves trapped. Accustomed to God's providential intervention, Moses remained calm. Precedent suggested that God would save them now. So Moses felt justified when he called out to the people to stand back and witness the salvation of the Lord.

To his surprise, the Bible records God's retort: "Why do you cry out to me? Speak to the children of Israel and tell them to go forward."

Heretofore, Moses was the face of the miracle to the people of Israel. Sure, miracles were ascribed to God, but only when Moses appeared on the scene did the miraculous event take place. Why wouldn't Moses come through again? Imagine their surprise, therefore, when they were told that they, not he, had to plunge headlong into the raging waters.

The people must have felt fear and outrage. Of course, no one wanted to take the first step. The one lonely chieftain, Nachshon, son of Aminadav, took the plunge, causing the waters to recede. All of us can picture what happened next.

Some scholars of various disciplines claim that the miracle of the parting of the raging sea was due to a tsunami produced by the explosion of a volcano, which caused the retreat of the waters, permitting the Israelites to cross over ahead of the Egyptians. Others have posited less dramatic oceanographic events, like strong winds that blew along the Gulf of Suez, pushing the waters back a considerable distance from the shoreline. Then, an abrupt shift of wind caused the waters to return to their previous position with a force that produced an instant flooding of the entire area.

If the broad outline of the biblical narratives can be believed, let us return to the description of the epic story: the Israelites found themselves in an impossible situation as they approached a large body of water, with the enemy in fast pursuit. Somehow, they escaped. Even if you cannot provide a precise scientific explanation for what happened, no one can deny the miraculous timing. Salvation arrived at the precise moment the Israelites needed it. For me, that in itself is a miracle!

In later biblical literature and many post biblical stories, miracles vary in size and scope but not necessarily in volume. The prophet Elijah and his disciple Elisha save lives with miracles. In the Talmud, the famed Honi, the Circle Maker, is able to help drought-plagued Palestine by bringing forth just the right amount of rain when needed. (Babylonian Talmud, Taanit 23a)

Many miracles portrayed in Talmudic and Hasidic literature take the form of cures or exorcisms. The founder of Hasidism, the Baal Shem Tov, ordered that a sick boy's soul should reenter the body and was able to send him on his way to a long life.

Occasionally, we read a tale that seems truly incredible. In the Talmud, we find the following account: "Our rabbis taught, once a man's wife died and left a child to be suckled and he could not afford to pay a wet nurse. Incredibly, a miracle was performed for him and his teats opened like two teats of a woman and he suckled his son."

When such dubious statements appear in the Talmud, they are usually attributed to a single individual. The fact that this story is introduced by "Our rabbis taught" indicates that they attached some credibility to this report. That's one miracle I would have liked to have seen!

For this man, milk in his breast meant everything. For the Israelites, the sticky white substance called manna sent to them in the desert was treated as an ultimate insult. These were the same people who witnessed the most incredible miracle that has ever taken place: the sea split, the Israelites were saved, the Egyptians drowned, then all sang songs of praise to God. Minutes later, however, all was forgotten because all they wanted to know is just one thing: "What's for lunch?" Surely, manna from heaven wasn't enough.

This story seems to underscore something I learned a long time ago: The impact of the miracle is much more limited than you might imagine, and its shelf life is even more limited. Maimonides makes the point that God never changes the nature of human beings by virtue of miracles.[60] In fact, the rabbis declare quite pointedly that the recipient of a miracle usually does not recognize the miracle! Interesting! We often don't know we are the beneficiary of the miracle! Perhaps it is true that miracles have to be seen to be believed, but they also have to be believed to be seen. Surely, that is the case for many people much of the time but certainly not for everybody all the time.

Miracles come at us from many directions and often find us when we least expect them. Sometimes, even, they seem to be communications from above. When my father-in-law collapsed and died suddenly in a North Carolina airport, his whole family was stunned. The night of his funeral, my wife and I sat on his bed, talking, crying, and reminiscing. Suddenly, a little string swirled above us. It caught our eye somehow, and for some reason, we continued to follow it. That string seemed to have a mind of its own. Suddenly, it hovered precisely over my father-in-law's pillow and twirled for what seemed like a solid minute. We couldn't believe what we were seeing, but we both saw this clearly. Without question, we thought this was a communication from Dad: "I'm all right. I will still be a part of your lives. Be strong."

My rabbinic colleague, Rabbi Camille Angel, told me that throughout her life, her mother had a love affair with birds. She would visit them, feed them, and even collect them on her shelf at home. Mom's husband and daughters tolerated her whimsical obsession. Years ago, her father died, and just recently her mom did as well. When the funeral procession pulled up to the cemetery, in front of their graves stood two white doves. No other birds were seen in the cemetery. At that point, Rabbi Angel knew that her parents' souls were reunited.

One more story: Stephen Feld was a young boy living in Poland. One day, he came home with a dire warning: the Nazis were coming to liquidate their village. Many residents simply could not fathom that happening. Stephen's own father and two siblings were taken away the very next day. Still in hiding, Stephen refused to accept the same fate and found a neighbor who was willing to hide him in his barn for a short time. That short time turned into several years, but Stephen never lost his life, his spirit, or his faith.

After coming to this country, Stephen became a cantor, somehow managing to sing praises to God in spite of all he had lived through. I will never forget that when two of his grandsons were called to the Torah at their B'nei Mitzvah, Cantor Feld announced their presence in a strong, unwavering voice. There was not a dry eye in the congregation. Throughout his ordeal, Stephen never lost his optimism and good humor. He was a true inspiration to all of us. Sadly, he died before his third grandson was called to the Torah at his Bar Mitzvah. The family was devastated and missed his presence terribly that day. His son Irwin had the following experience, which he conveyed to me in an e-mail:

Dear Robert,

The other day I was driving in my car tired after a long day. I flipped around the radio stations hoping to catch the market reports or headlines. My search landed at the end of the dial where I was nearly deafened by the sound of static, only to hear the voice of a cantor coming through. My first thought was, "Oh, my dad would love this." Somehow I was captivated by the voice of this man. The melody he sang was so reminiscent of the style of my father so many years ago. His pathos and emotion had me gripping the wheel so tightly; the car seemed to be going on autopilot.

When I heard those high notes, they did not sound like my father's, they *were* my father's notes. I looked ahead in the sky and there was this enormous white streak that appeared to divide the sky in half. On one side was some high clouds, the other was clear blue. The voice grew dim. I wanted so much to hear the singing. My father is up there somewhere doing what he loved to do best. After the initial shock, I found some comfort knowing he's spending eternity filling the heavens with his gift for song. I have tuned into that station every day since. It plays only Latin music.

How do such seemingly incredible occurrences happen? Are they somehow built into the master plan for the universe and brought to the fore at their "appropriate" time? Our ancestors were as concerned about this question as we are and often battled each other. According to Maimonides, miracles are predetermined at the time of creation and constitute most unusual but not unforeseen happenings. The medieval philosopher Nahmanides disagreed, saying, "Events like rain coming precisely when it's needed or victory in battle over incredibly overwhelming odds, are miracles and are not predetermined." Buber contends that the miracle is "Our receptivity to the eternal revelation."[61]

Obviously, it is hard to know for sure. The bigger question in my mind is, how much should we care about miracles, given the fact that they are usually episodic, fleeting, and have little lasting effect?

Perhaps we need to care less about the momentary miracle and more about the miracles that have longer-lasting effects. Rabbi Herbert Baumgard gave a memorable sermon in which he talked about the everyday miracles, like childbirth:

> Is the miracle of birth the product of a deviation from the natural order as created by God or is it the direct result of the process that God created which He still feeds with His power...
>
> Recently I saw a movie which describes the in utero process of a child's birth...The chances of the semen reaching the egg are miniscule, so God has provided that there are countless numbers of live sperm, only one of which succeeds in reaching the egg. Then you see the fertilized egg subdivide, and the long and miraculous process of subdivision of cells and development begins. From the one cell many cells are formed, each identical

to the other; and yet, somewhere down the line, the identical cells, each with the same potential to be anything else, begin to form specific parts of the child's body...

How do these cells know which part of the body is assigned to them? How do they know how to convert the specific program or potential which exists within them? Who or what gives the signal for the cell to become active and differentiated? It is a miracle or series of miracles which none understands as yet and still it is an orderly process, so orderly that it seldom fails...

A thousand miracles are revealed from one tiny cell. Is this not proof enough of a Master planner! What need have I to believe that God is manifest only in the deviations from nature? It is the order of nature which proves God best![62]

In my view, the fact that the Jewish people and Jewish faith, to which I have devoted my life, are still alive and vibrant despite countless attempts from Pharaoh to Haman to Hitler to consign us to the dustbins of history is truly incredible. Rabbi Steinberg wrote poignantly of this miracle:

There is an old wonder, centuries old...a quiet, unspectacular wonder, therefore we pay it no heed...If we could transport ourselves in imagination back to the year seventy and stand where Israel stood then, after its dreadful defeat in the war with Rome; one-fifth of its numbers dead; another fifth sold into slavery; the land lost, the Temple lost, the Sanhedrin lost, the schools lost, everything lost. What odds would be given for the survival of this people? Had there ever been till then, would there be in all of history, a single instance of a people living without its land, let alone after such vast losses?

Then suppose that in the nineteen centuries since then to the present this people were subjected to massacre, expulsion, expropriation, to every conceivable cruelty, humiliation, and disability

166

at the hand of every nation, church, class among whom it sought refuge...The great Russian theologian Nicholas Berdyaev pronounced bluntly: "The continued existence of Jewry down the centuries is rationally inexplicable."[63]

Rabbi Alexander Schindler adds: "This too is an unprecedented event in human history: that a state which had passed out of existence should recreate itself two thousand years later! Who of all the powerful empires that conquered ancient Israel would ever have dreamed their own extinction would be accentuated by the rebirth of the Jewish homeland? Rome fell and remains fallen. Babylon fell and remains fallen. Assyria fell and remains fallen. But the Jewish people lives and the Jewish State was reborn."[64]

Yes, the survival of the Jewish people is a miracle for which I do not have a rational explanation. About four thousand years ago, according to the Bible, God promised that a covenant between a God and a people would be eternal. Today, we are still very much here. That is what I know, and it's indisputable.

In my judgment, then, there are miracles big and small all around us, and there always have been. Ultimately, what matters is not how they happen, why, or by whom. In the end, what matters is how these miracles change us. To suggest that there is a possible existence of miracles is to say that everything that happens in the world is not in our control. Ultimately, we are not the center of the universe. Acknowledgment of miracles should make us more grateful and generous of spirit, open to other people and their needs. Whether or not they all come from God, miracles can make us more human and convince us that just as in the time of Moses and Jesus, we can't just sit back and wait for God to swoop down and perform for us. To effect the miracle, we have to be active participants, partners perhaps, making the miraculous possible. By acting in this manner, we may or may not change the world around us, but we will be forever changed for the better.

Let me share the story of the child who developed the custom of walking in the woods every day. His father became concerned and wondered why he wanted to venture into such a dark, dangerous place.

"Why do you go there every day?" his dad asked.

"I go there to speak with God."

"But, Son, God is the same everywhere."

"But I'm not the same."

Knowing that the miraculous is possible, you and I will never be the same again either.

# CHAPTER TWELVE

⌒

# How We Can Believe in God Today

**M**Y RELATIONSHIP TO GOD OBVIOUSLY did not end one Passover night. Sitting around the Seder table, I was too young to realize that all relationships that truly matter never just banish from our lives. Even those people from whom we are estranged get carried around in our minds and tug at our hearts, causing us to think and fret more often than we might care to admit. Of course, these are bonds that one day might be repaired by picking up the phone or pressing send on an e-mail. Relationships with a power we cannot see or readily talk to are quite a bit more difficult to reconcile and even understand.

Because we cannot text-message God or download a deity from MySpace, the purpose of this book is not to prove or convince you that God exists and is a force in your life. My goal is not even to convince you that God lives.

My hope, simply, is that you will be more open to God now than before you started this book. My rabbinic colleague, Rabbi Samuel Karff, once wrote that there is "a believer and an unbeliever in each of us."[65] The rabbi may very well be right, but the vast majority of the people I have met want not only to believe in God but to have God matter in their lives.

That is why I have refrained from personally embracing the broad theological diversity in Western religion. God as the highest ideal, the unmoved mover, streams of divine light, naturalistic power—all may legitimately be viewed as authentic ways to believe in God, but they don't give us that personal relationship that can matter to both parties. The Torah, the New Testament, and the Quran clearly teach us that God entered the world precisely to have that kind of connection with human beings. In many ways, God needs a divine-human interaction as much as we do.

Knowing that God is dependent on us to some degree may help us let our guard down, reduce our natural cynicism, and realize how crucial God is to our perspective on living. As Rabbi Jacob Philip Rudin once said in a memorable sermon:

> We need God. We need the hope which comes from Him...We need God for the sense of timelessness beyond our time, for the sense of eternity to cradle our brief hours.
>
> We need His arms to uphold us.
>
> We need His presence to know that the world eternally has a place for memory and for life whose years are ended.

Need is one of those never-to-be-spoken four-letter words when talking about faith. Need opens the believers to the familiar bromide that "God didn't make man; man made God." God, some will say, is a human construct born of human weakness.

Pity the people who need nothing or no one in their lives. Need is not a human weakness; on the contrary, it is courageous to admit that you need others in your life. Connecting to others this way makes us more productive and fulfilled, makes us feel better about ourselves, and allows us to extend a helping hand in the direction of our neighbors. Mutual need is a win-win proposition.

So, let me admit to you right here, right now, that I *need* God. However, my belief in God does not come from any perceived weakness within but from everything I can see and perceive very much outside of myself. My belief ultimately overwhelmed my doubts because of the simple fact I have been stunned again and again in my life by experiences that I cannot understand any way other than that God lives in our world and in my life. Even after I hear all the rational, logical, scientific explanations, I am still in awe.

When each of my children was conceived and born, I was stunned.

When the doctors told my parents I would probably not be able to walk and would likely be mentally impaired and then I grew upright and was able to talk a blue streak as a rabbi, I was stunned.

That the Jewish people have survived and thrived as a faith group for close to four thousand years despite numerous efforts to destroy us and a history where so many other peoples and civilizations far more powerful than ours have disappeared, I am stunned.

I am stunned by the fact that I can wake up each new day without falling off the face of the Earth.

I am stunned by evolution and natural selection.

I am stunned by human resiliency. Time after time, I see people filled with grief, so heartbroken that they swear they can't go on. Nothing in their lives heretofore indicates an ability to summon the courage to pick themselves up from unspeakable tragedy, then go on and live an active, productive life. Truly, I believe that God gave them the strength to persevere.

171

That's all well and good, you may be saying, but I'm a very visual person. Seeing is believing. Interestingly, the Torah depicts Moses feeling the exact same way. After descending the mountain, carrying the tablets of the law, he is devastated by the sight of his people dancing around the golden calf, which appeared to Moses as an idolatrous violation of the covenant. Impulsively, he smashes the tablets over them and puts to death thousands of violators.

Feeling very much alone, Moses ascends the mountain again as shattered as the tablets. No way can he continue leading his people unless he absolutely knows that God is with him. Moses now demands something he hadn't asked before: a concrete manifestation of God's existence, visual proof that God truly is an active presence in their world.

"No one can see my face and live," answers God, "but I will make my goodness pass before you." God's answer may have disappointed a desperate Moses at that moment, but it is the answer that has lived through the ages. You can't see me, God is saying, but you will know that I am here because of what I do.

Sensing Moses's disappointment and feeling the gravity of the situation, God makes an extraordinary concession to this man who has devoted his entire life to the divine-human relationship: "Stand upon that rock! It shall come to pass that I'll put thee in a cleft of the rock and will cover thee until I have passed by. And you shall see my achorai, but my face you will not be able to see."

Most bibles translate *achorai* as "back" (you shall see my back), but that is an anthropomorphic misunderstanding of the text's intentions. More accurately, we can translate the Hebrew to read "And you shall see my aftermath." Moses knew God was there only after God had passed by. You and I can learn an important lesson from Moses's remarkable experience because if Moses will never see God right in front of him, rest assured that neither shall we. Yet, we, too, can know God has been here by seeing the results, by looking back and understanding that whether or not he knew it at the time, God was here!

Clearly, God was present the night Sally Kaplan called my study from Memorial Sloan-Kettering Hospital. Her husband Peter was failing from a rare cancer, which he had been battling heroically. To make matters even more painful, their daughter Emily was going to have her Bat Mitzvah in about six months. Sally knew that Peter would not live to see their daughter bask in the glow of that day. Our plan had been to hold a small Bat Mitzvah enactment as soon as Peter was able to get home.

Unexpectedly, Peter's condition suddenly deteriorated, and he was not expected to survive the night. I ran down to the sanctuary, opened the ark, grabbed a Torah scroll, and hailed a cab. Time permitting, Emily would be called to the Torah, would have a Bat Mitzvah with her father in the hospital room that very night.

Emily and I huddled in the lounge for a quick review. Perfect Hebrew pronunciation was far less the focus than was preparing this lovely girl emotionally for her life-affirming ritual at death's door.

"Ready?" I asked. Emily's ashen face barely registered a response.

Sally greeted us at the door with her usual beautiful smile, but Peter surprised me. He was sitting up in bed, talking and quipping, quite animated. As the service flowed, I couldn't help but notice that Peter sang with a rare gusto. He was so present to his wife, daughter, and son Teddy, there was no doubt in my mind that holiness pervaded that usually grim space. Peter, Sally, and Teddy chanted the traditional Torah blessing, then Emily did. This family, struck by tragic illness, felt really blessed to have this night, to be able to convey both in words and silent affirmation all they meant to each other.

"I'm so proud of you, Emmy," Peter said loudly and proudly. This would become the blessing from parent to child that Emily could carry with her for the rest of her life. "I love you," he called out as Emily left the room.

Peter died that very night. In my mind, God was fully present from the time Sally picked up the phone to call me until the moment Peter died and ever since. In the weeks and months ahead, Sally went on to study God's role in this world and beyond and to begin a most meaningful career in spiritual care. I'll never forget the day she gave the keynote address in front of doctors and clergy on the role of pastoral care in her life and in theirs. With true courage, she spoke of that special night and how it had changed her forever. Whether she was fully aware during that last incredible, fateful night of Peter's life, she was now as certain as any human being could be that God had been there with them and for them, helping their family receive God's blessing through the lips of Peter Kaplan during that unforgettable Bat Mitzvah service.

Many people report feeling God's powerful presence in the aftermath. That is what people were trying to say to me on my book tour—that they felt God most intensely not at a moment of great joy and blessing but in the midst of tragedy and grief, when they were felled by life and had no idea how to get up, when they were convinced that they did not have the strength to go on.

Incredibly, some told me, there was some invisible force that kept them from going under, which gave them the strength to survive and find life again.

"Yea, though I walk in the valley of the shadow of death," the 23rd Psalm reads, "I shall fear no evil for God is with me." In the deepest valley, people often know God is there. Thus, they find the courage to get through the darkness because they find out at that crucial moment that, indeed, they are not alone.

When Rabbi Steinberg stepped outside after a brief illness, he was overawed by the sunlight, and as he basked in this "glory of a golden flood," he resolved to give thanks to the God who "gives us so much of which we are careless."

You can find God in the darkness. You can find God in the light. You can find God in the aftermath. But you have to be open to the revelation. As a wise Hasidic teacher once said, "There's no room for God in people who are too full of themselves."

Let me once more address any lingering doubts:

*I'm too scientific to believe in God.* Science really is very compatible with God. Science attempts to answer the how but can never answer the why. As you have read, many scientists and many atheists are filled with wonder over why things happen. Wonder is the crucial cornerstone of belief.

*If there was a God, there would be no suffering.* No one was put on this Earth to enjoy a pain-free existence. That is not part of the contract. The covenant guarantees that you'll not be alone in your struggle and makes us responsible to ease the pain of others. In my experience, the best way to stop hurting is to start helping someone else stop hurting.

*Look what people do in the name of religion.* Too many people invoke God's name to justify all kinds of horrible things, including barbaric killings. So did Hitler.

God is not responsible for what people do in God's name. Religion is not responsible for what people do in the name of religion.

*I still think that man created God—not the other way around.* Most people experience God not by sitting around and channeling God into their worldview. Rather, we find God along the way and often when we least expect the encounter. Try this simple experiment: Tomorrow morning, say, "Thank you" for one blessing. You don't even have to go to a house of worship, you don't even have to use the word *God*. Just say, "Thanks." Then, do one kindness for one person. Do that for a week. See if your perspective changes, whether you feel at all differently about the existence and presence of God.

I'll let you in on a secret the Bible taught us thousands of years ago. If you turn to the Book of Deuteronomy, Chapter 6, you will find a central prayer of Jewish liturgy called the Sh'ma. The first line reads:

Hear O Israel, the Lord is our God, the Lord is One.

This is the Jewish people's quintessential statement of faith. Curiously, one chapter before, we read the Ten Commandments, which provide the concise action plan for God's human partners. You might think that first you have to have faith in order to understand why you're doing what you're doing and that belief leads to action. Actually, the reverse is true. When we first act as if there is a God in the world, we will come to understand that God exists. In that context, belief in God becomes plausible.

The Bible's simple answer then is: Start doing.

Call a sick friend. Shop for someone homebound. Bring food to a pantry and fill the bags that will help a hungry family get through the month. Volunteer at a homeless shelter to help a fellow human being get through the night. Simply put, live as if there is a God, and you will find your belief. Quite likely, you will discover your God.

Act first, believe later. That is a compelling message, but not every biblical persona wanted to follow such a plan. The prophet Jonah was a prime example. Jonah was commanded to do something important—go to the city of the mighty Assyrian oppressor, Nineveh, and warn them of their impending doom if they did not change their evil ways. Jonah sought their death and defied the deity. Turning his back on God's command, he boarded a ship, was summarily thrown overboard, and was then swallowed by a great fish, which then vomited him out, fully intact. Chastened, he begrudgingly agreed to answer God's command.

The prophet goes to Nineveh and succeeds in his mission, as the entire populous actually repents. Jonah is distraught because he never wanted this wicked nation to repent from their evil ways.

Needing the prophet to act in His name, God decides to teach Jonah a lesson by placing a shady tree over his head, then causing it to wither away. Suffering in the blazing heat, Jonah cries out in self-pity and remorse for the plant.

Seizing the heated moment, God tells Jonah: "You had pity on the gourd for which you did not labor nor make grow, which arose within one night and perished within one night. Shall I not spare Nineveh, that great city, where there is some six thousand people who can't tell the difference between their right hand and their left, plus much cattle?"

The Book of Jonah evokes God's compassion for all people with the intent to give them a second chance.

Notice, however, that God does not wait for a response. This is the only Book in Scriptures that ends with a question. In this case, the question mark is not a literary device nor is it placed there to leave us in suspense.

God doesn't wait for an answer because He doesn't want to hear from the prophet. God is expecting not to dialogue but for the prophet to continue his mission.

No concern is voiced here for what Jonah feels. Rather, he is expected to do what he is placed on Earth to do. In this fascinating tale, we, along with Jonah, learn God's great lesson to humankind:

> You are not what you feel.
> You are not what you intend.
> You are not what you believe.
> *You are what you do.*

Now I'm going to shock you. Just as God cares a whole lot less about our feelings than our actions, I really believe that God cares a whole lot less about whether you believe in God than whether you act as if you do. If you do what the Bible teaches, if you attempt to act on the commandment "You shall be holy, for I, the Eternal, am holy," you have fulfilled your role. Please note that as explanation for the commandment to be holy, the text does not instruct us to go up on the mountain or flee into the forest in order to commune spiritually. That's not what holiness means. Holiness is an action plan that sends us back into the messiness of the real world in order to make a difference there.

> And when you reap the harvest of your land, thou shall not wholly reap the corners of thy field, neither shall thou gather the gleanings of thy harvest...thou shall leave them for the poor and stranger: I am the Lord, your God...thou shall not defraud thy neighbor nor rob him; the wages of him that is higher shall not abide with thee all night until the morning...thou shall not go up and down as a tale bearer among thy people; neither shall thy stand idle while thy neighbor bleeds. I am the Lord...thou shall love thy neighbor as thyself; I am the Lord. (Leviticus 19)

As Rabbi Harold Schulweis put it so well: "Jewish holiness is not a global, abstract feeling of awe or mystery, an uncanny meditation on an isolated mountaintop. Jewish holiness takes one out of solitariness into community, out of the cosmetics of beauty into the grim and dust of the marketplace...Holiness is not a 'what'; it is a 'with.' Jewish holiness is in relationship with the broken vessels of society: the poor, the stranger, the fatherless, the widow...It takes place in the marketplace, the prison, the hospital, the convalescent home.[66]

The quest for holiness gets us into places God would appear if God actually walked among us. There, we will come face to face with pain we otherwise wouldn't see, which helps us to quickly forget our own. When we look into those eyes and do something to repair a situation, a wounded body, or broken heart, we will see the image of God looking back at us. At that moment, they will know that they are not alone, and you will know that you are not alone.

The story is told of two brothers, Rabbi Elimelech and Rabbi Susha, who spent many years as itinerant preachers and teachers, trying to reach as many people as they could. Once, when they arrived in a town, Rabbi Susha announced that his brother would deliver a sermon that evening, whose wisdom would inspire everyone. But the sermon disappointed them, and his remarks left them cold. At that moment, Rabbi Susha stood up and told the following story:

> A businessman traveling to Leipzig brought a new coffee urn and told the woman in charge that henceforth she would not have to kindle the stove to heat the coffee. All she would have to do is blow a few minutes and a fire would heat the water.
>
> The following morning, the maid filled the urn with water and began to blow—but in vain. It seemed like a hoax until the man explained that he meant the fire had to be started with charcoal, which could be fanned easily by blowing.

Rabbi Susha explained: "My brother can fan the flame only if there is a spark, but he's helpless when the last spark is extinguished."

So it is with God. God has put us on this Earth to be His eyes and ears, to reflect not only God's will but God's soul in the world. God can only be fully God if we rise to our fullest potential, if we provide the spark.

Don't wait for a thunderbolt or certainty to come over you. You will wait forever. Belief in God is hard to achieve. Rabbi Lawrence Kushner suggests that as we climb the ladder of holy awareness and as God descends the same ladder, each arrives at his or her destination "a thin diluted version of what once started out."[67]

He may be right, but we need to try. Our lives and the world may very well depend upon our efforts. So, start climbing. Act as if there is a God. Do something that shows real caring for others. Try prayer, study, meditation, dance, anything that will make you aware of spiritual realms around and above you. Whatever you try, never fail to do, never fail to act holy. When you are happy and when you are devastated, act as if you were created in the image of God. Particularly when you are devastated.

Rabbi Heschel concludes his book *Man's Quest for God: Studies in Prayer and Symbolism* with this story:

> A learned man lost all his sources of income and was looking for a way to earn a living. The members of his community, who admired him for his learning and piety, suggested that he serve as their cantor on the Days of Awe. But he considered himself unworthy of serving...as the one who should bring the prayers of his fellow-men to the Almighty. He went to his master, the Rabbi of Husiatin, and told him...of the invitation to serve as cantor on the Days of Awe, and of his being afraid to accept it and to pray for the congregation.
>
> "Be afraid, and pray," was the answer of the rabbi.[68]

So it's not at all unusual to approach spiritual matters on shaky ground with shaky hands. It is fine not to be certain, even fine to be afraid.

Be afraid and pray. Be afraid and believe. Be afraid, and act as if there is a God in the world. Then, neither you nor God will be alone. Together, you can make a better world and a better you.

# ENDNOTES

1. Elie Wiesel, *Night* (New York: Bantam Books, 1982).
2. Jeffery L. Sheler, *Believers A Journey Into Evangelical America* (New York: Viking, 2006) 22–25.
3. Ibid. 5.
4. Karen Armstrong, *A Prophet For Our Time* (New York: Harper Collins, 2006) 45–46.
5. Cheyenne Indian prayer, http://www.worldprayers.org/frameit.cgi?/archive/prayers/invocations/oh_great_spirit_who se_voice.html.
6. Jacob Berkman, "Prayer group uses 'Jam Davening' for a more spiritual experience," Jewish Telegraphic Agency (December 11, 2007), http://www.jta.org/cgi-bin/iowa/news/article/2007121120071211jamdaven.html, accessed January 18, 2008.
7. Carolyn Stearns, "The Song Finally Sung," Pilgrimage Press, Vol. 26, 2001/2002, http://www.pilgrimagepress.org/bestof/song.htm, accessed January 18, 2008.

8. Navajo chant, holisticonline.com, "Selected Prayers," http://www.1stholistic.com/Spl_prayers/prayer_navaho-chant.htm, accessed January 18, 2008.

9. Milton Steinberg, *Anatomy of Faith* (New York: Harcourt, Brace & Company, 1960), 91–93.

10. Kevin Phillips, *American Theocracy: The Peril and Politics of Radical Religion, Oil and Borrowed Money in the 21st Century* (New York: Viking, 2006), 102.

11. Christine Rosen, *My Fundamentalist Education: A Memoir of a Divine Girlhood* (New York: PublicAffairs, 2005), 79.

12. Phillips, *American Theocracy*, 26.

13. Rosen, *My Fundamentalist Education*, 126.

14. Richard Dawkins, *The God Delusion* (Massachusetts: Houghton Mifflin, 2006), 31.

15. Ibid., 245.

16. Sam Harris, *The End of Faith: Religion, Terror, and the Future of Reason* (New York: W. W. Norton & Company, 2004), 127.

17. Sam Harris, *Letters to a Christian Nation* (New York: Knopf, 2006), 85.

18. Dawkins, *The God Delusion*, 308.

19. Ibid., 366–367.

20. Harris, *The End of Faith*, 227.

21. Sam Harris, *Letters to a Christian Nation*, 87–88.

22. Rabbi Marcia Prager, *The Path of Blessing* (Woodstock, VT: Jewish Lights Publishing, 2003), 130–134.

23. Walter Isaacson, "Einstein & Faith," *Time*, April 2007, http://www.time.com/time/magazine/article/0,9171,1607298,00.html, accessed March 7, 2008.

24. Alan Lightman, "The Power of Mysteries," National Public Radio, November 25, 2005, http://www.prx.org/pieces/10917, accessed March 7, 2008.

25. Isadore Twersky, *A Maimonides Reader*, "Letter on Astrology" (New York: Behrman House), 1972.

26. Moses Maimonides, *The Guide for the Perplexed,* II:1.

27. Kenneth Chang, "How Did the Universe Survive the Big Bang? In This Experiment, Clues Remain Elusive," *New York Times,* April 12, 2007.

28. Dr. Francis Collins, "Scientists Speak Up on Mix of God and Science," *New York Times,* August 23, 2005.

29. Debra Nussbaum Cohen, Jewish Telegraphic Agency, March 20, 2007.

30. Intro by Milton Himmelfarb, "The State of Jewish Belief, A Symposium," *Commentary Magazine,* August 1966.

31. Eliezar Berkowitz, Ibid., 79.

32. Yoel Teitelbaum Sefer Va-yoel Moshe, reprinted in *Judaism,* edited by Arthur Herzberg (New York: Simon and Schuster, 1991), 265.

33. Elie Wiesel, *Beggar in Jerusalem* (New York: Avon Books, 1970), 140–141.

34. Elie Wiesel, *Legends of Our Time* (New York: Henry Holt and Company, 1968), 186.

35. "How Do You Know There Is a God?" questionnaire, *The American Rabbi, Pastoral Services,* December 1993.

36. Charles Taylor, *A Secular Age* (Cambridge, MA: Belknap Press, 2007), 302.

37. Jack Miles, *God: A Biography* (New York: Vintage Books, 1995), 328.

38. Ibid., 408.

39. Søren Kierkegaard, *Fear and Trembling and Sickness Unto Death,* translated with introduction and notes by Walter Lowrie (Princeton, NJ: Princeton University Press, 1954), 59.

40. Ibid., 38.

41. David Rankin, "Growing Up With God," *American Rabbi, Pastoral Services,* April 1990.

42. Milton Steinberg, *A Believing Jew* (New York: Harcourt, Brace and Company, 1951), 316.

43. Rhonda Byrne, *The Secret* (New York: Atria Books/Beyond Words, 2006), 183.

44. Ibid.

45. Steven Levy and Brad Stone, "The New Wisdom of the Web," *Newsweek*, April 3, 2006.

46. Tom Friedman, "The Whole World Is Watching," *New York Times,* June 27, 2007.

47. Donald J. Moore, *Martin Buber Prophet of Religious Secularism,* (New York: Fordham University Press, 1996) p. xxvi (as quoted in *Bucher und Menschen in Hinweise: Gesammelte Essays* (Aurich:Manesse Verlag, 1953)

48. Milton Steinberg, *To Hold With Open Arms,* Sidney Greenberg, *Treasury of Comfort* (California: Wilshire Book Company, 1978), 272–273.

49. Sidney Greenberg, *Hidden Hungers: High Holiday Sermons on the Art of Living* (Indianapolis: Hartman House, 1972), 101.

50. Harold Kushner, *When All You've Ever Wanted Isn't Enough* (New York: Summit Books, 1986) 146.

51. Chaim Stern, *Gates of Prayer* (New York: Central Conference of American Rabbis).

52. Jim Bishop, "There Is No God..." *The Olean Times Herald* (Olean, NY), February 20, 1963.

53. Dr. Sanjay Gupta, "Remembering a Miracle," CNN.com, April 06, 2007, http://www.cnn.com/HEALTH/blogs/ paging.dr.gupta/archive/2007_04_01_archive.html, accessed October 6, 2007.

54. Alan Dershowitz, *Blasphemy: How the Religious Right Is Hijacking the Declaration of Independence* (New York: Wiley, 2007), 67.

55. Phillips, *American Theocracy,* 105.

56. Ibid., 123.

57. Josephus, *Antiquities of the Jews,* 17:295.

58. Kenneth Woodward, *The Book of Miracles* (New York: A Touchstone Book, 2000), 28.

59. Lawrence Kushner, *Eyes Remade for Wonder: A Kushner Reader* (Woodstock, VT: Jewish Lights Publishing, 1998), 63–65.

60. (*Guide to the Perplexed,* 3:32)

61. (Moses, 1958, p. 66 and ff)

62. Herbert M. Baumgard, "Do You Believe in Miracles?" *The American Rabbi,* February 1986.

63. Steinberg, *A Believing Jew,* 200–201.

64. Alexander Schindler, "The Jewish Century," *Achim, North American Federation of Temple Brotherhoods,* Spring 2001.

65. Samuel Egal Karff, "Experiencing God's Presence," *Sermons from the Beth Israel Pulpit, 1998–1999* (Texas: Congregation Beth Israel, 1999).

66. Rabbi Harold Schulweis, *Moment Magazine,* October 1986.

67. Kushner, *Eyes Remade for Wonder,* 181.

68. Abraham Joshua Heschel, "Man's Quest for God: Studies in Prayer and Symbolism," reprinted in *Moment Magazine,* October 1990.

# INDEX

# ABOUT THE AUTHOR

**Rabbi Robert Levine** leads Congregation
Rodeph Sholom, one of the largest reform
synagogues in New York. He has been the
president of the New York Board of Rabbis,
Chairman of the Catholic-Jewish Dialogue
of the Archdiocese of New York, and one of
New York's most active interfaith cler-
gymen. He has played a significant role in
restoring millions of dollars to New York
City centers for the homeless and other

© Richard Lobell Photography

services. A frequent television guest, he has appeared on CNN's
*Paula Zahn Now*, CNN's *Crossfire*, and CBS's *The Early Show*. He is
the author of *Where Are You When I Need You?: Befriending God
When Life Hurts* and *There is No Messiah and You're It: The Stunning
Transformation of Judaism's Most Provocative Idea*.